Charles T. Leigh
Endowed Memorial Fund

THIS BOOK WAS PRESENTED
TO THE
W. H. ABEL MEMORIAL LIBRARY BY
R. H. FLEET
IN FOND MEMORY OF HIS FRIEND,

Charles T. Leigh

Timberland Regional Library
Service Center
415 Tumwater Blvd. SW
Tumwater, WA 98501

AUG 1 8 2004

CLASSIC Chevrolet DEALERSHIPS

SELLING THE BOWTIE

JON G. ROBINSON

MOTORBOOKS
INTERNATIONAL

Dedication

For Brad Bowling, my first editor.

I'll never misspell "asparagus" again!

This edition first published in 2003 by Motorbooks International, an imprint of MBI Publishing Company, Galtier Plaza, Suite 200, 380 Jackson Street, St. Paul, MN 55101-3885 USA

© Jon G. Robinson, 2003

All rights reserved. With the exception of quoting brief passages for the purposes of review, no part of this publication may be reproduced without prior written permission from the Publisher.

The information in this book is true and complete to the best of our knowledge. All recommendations are made without any guarantee on the part of the author or Publisher, who also disclaim any liability incurred in connection with the use of this data or specific details.

We recognize that some words, model names and designations, for example, mentioned herein are the property of the trademark holder. We use them for identification purposes only. This is not an official publication. Motorbooks International titles are also available at discounts in bulk quantity for industrial or sales-promotional use. For details write to Special Sales Manager at Motorbooks International Wholesalers & Distributors, Galtier Plaza, Suite 200, 380 Jackson Street, St. Paul, MN 55101-3885 USA.

ISBN 0-7603-1439-X

On the front cover, top: Webster Chevrolet; Cody, Wyoming. **Bottom:** Holz Motors; Hales Corners, Wisconsin.

On the frontispiece: *Bob McDorman collection*

On the title page: Cox Motor Company; Bradenton, Florida.

On the back cover, left: Felix Chevrolet; Los Angeles, California. **Right:** Cox Motor Company; Bradenton, Florida.

Editor: Amy Glaser
Designer: LeAnn Kuhlmann

Printed in Hong Kong

Contents

Acknowledgments

To all the people who contributed to this book in large and small ways: Thank you!

General Motors regional managers: Dave Klemm, Steve Beltz, Jay Allen, Brian Brockman, Dan Hubbert, Mark Drennan, Scott Osborn, Bill Beasley. **General Motors Communications**: Tom Wilkinson, Nancy Libby, Mary Roberts, Ron Updyke, Michael Albano, Craig Eppling.

At the dealerships: **Whitney's Chevrolet, Montesano, Washington**: Stormy Glick; Les Foss; the late Forest Kelsey; John Larson, Polson Museum, Hoquiam, Washington; Craig Murphy, the *Vidette* newspaper, Montesano, Washington. **William L. Morris Chevrolet, Fillmore, California**: The late William L. Morris, John Chapman Morris Sr., John Chapman Morris Jr., Bill Morris. **Felix Chevrolet, Los Angeles, California**: Nick Shammas, Susan Sarff, Norman Bent, Assad Farah. **Mandeville Chevrolet, North Attleboro, Massachusetts**: Ron Mandeville, Lucille Mandeville Benoit. **Webster Chevrolet, Cody, Wyoming**: Bud Webster. **Culberson-Stowers Chevrolet, Pampa, Texas**: Dick and Dorothy Stowers, Richard Stowers. **Smith Chevrolet, Atlanta, Georgia**: Hal Smith, John Smith. **Holz Motors, Hales Corners, Wisconsin**: Jerry Holz.

To the members of the Holler family and their assistants for help with William Holler and his Quality Dealer Program: Roger Holler, Chris Holler, Sheri Aponte.

To the dealerships who made great efforts to share their photo archives: **City Chevrolet, Great Falls, Montana**: Leslie Oakland. **Cox Chevrolet, Bradenton, Florida**: Steve Cox, Tammy Cox. **Dimmitt Chevrolet, Clearwater, Florida**: Larry Dimmitt Jr., Larry Dimmitt III, Bonnie Kopcik. **Ferman Chevrolet, Tampa, Florida**: Frank North. **O'Rielly Chevrolet, Tucson, Arizona**: Buck O'Rielly, Gail Stewart. **Southern Arizona Auto Company, Douglas, Arizona**: Bill Mason. **Blanck Chevrolet, Brownsburg, Indiana**: Dave Blanck.

For help with special articles: **1953 Dealer Agreement**: Keith Hill, Illinois. **Advance Design Trucks**: Jim Hinckley, Arizona; Bill Morris, William L. Morris Chevrolet. **1942 Chevrolet Dealer Album**: Tom Meleo, California. **1954 Chevrolet Sales Materials**: Keith Hill, Illinois. **Jim Meagher, The Occasional Lemon**: Tim Meagher, Mickey Schreiner. **OK Used Cars**: Bob McDorman, McDorman Chevrolet, Canal Winchester, Ohio. **Laws, Dealers, and the Continuing Debate**: Bud Webster, Webster Chevrolet, Cody, Wyoming; Cornell Law School, The Legal Information Institute, U.S. Code Collection website; University of Arizona, James E. Rogers College of Law, Law Library website. *Fingertip Facts for the 1955 Chevrolet:* Fred Lossman, California. **Chevrolet Promotional Models**: Kurtis Brown, Michigan.

For help with the city profiles in Part 3: **St. Francis Dam disaster**: Don Ray, author and oral historian; Santa Clarita Valley Historical Society website. **Grays Harbor, Washington**: Patty Clemmons and Mary Shane, Chehalis Valley Historical Society, Montesano, Washington; John Larson, Polson Museum, Hoquiam, Washington. **Big Horn Basin, Wyoming**: Jeannie Cook, Park County Historical Society; Buffalo Bill Historical Center, Cody, Wyoming. **North Attleboro, Massachusetts**: George Cunningham, Falls Fire Barn Museum, North Attleboro, Massachusetts; Chuck Arning, John H. Chafee Blackstone River Valley National Heritage Corridor. **Dust Bowl**: Anne Davidson, White Deer Land Museum, Pampa, Texas; Rodger Harris, Oklahoma Historical Society, Oklahoma City, Oklahoma. **Los Angeles history**: Alan Barasorda, Los Angeles Conservancy; Bob Blew, Historical Society of Southern California; Morgan Yates, Automobile Club of Southern California, Los Angeles, California. **Milwaukee Electric Railway and Light Company**: Larry Sakar, electric railroad historian. **Atlanta history**: Don Rooney, Atlanta History Center.

Special thanks to all those who conducted photography: Brad Bowling, Marc Mirabile, Jamie Kelly, Jason Egbert.

Big thanks to **Tom Meleo** for letting me drag my photographic lights all over his outstanding collection of Chevrolets and Bowtie memorabilia, and to Chevrolet collector and historian **Pinky Randall** for some difficult and time-consuming help with research. Thank you also to **Mark Patrick** of the Detroit Public Library.

Thanks to **Steve Anderson** for travel and photography help.

A big thank you to the whole crew of **NAPA Auto Parts, Hesperia, California,** to the engineers and factory people who built the 1950 DeSoto that carried me the 10,000 miles it took to write this book, and to makers of coffee and fine Scotch whiskey everywhere.

Introduction

The Apology

In the nineteenth century, North America was settled by the horse, the wagon, and the steam engine. In the twentieth century, the continent was tamed further by the station wagon, the pickup truck, and the U.S. highway. It's time to write down the memories and thoughts of those who pioneered the new automotive frontier.

History commonly records the actions of military generals, but it doesn't always tell the harrowing stories of the common soldiers on the front lines. Similarly, the names of the American auto industry's founding generals are well known—David Buick, Ransom Olds, Henry Ford, Charles Nash, Walter Chrysler, John and Horace Dodge, among many others. The dealers were the common soldiers on the front lines of the auto industry's most delicate battle—the fight between the manufacturers and the public. The dealers were needed and resented, respected and spit on, and helped and hurt by both the car makes and the car buyers. The manufacturers were giant corporations, but the dealerships were family businesses—intrepid entrepreneurs exercising their right to work for themselves. They were the American "little guys" in spite of having a giant corporate logo looming above their showrooms.

Chevrolet started out as just another risky new enterprise in 1912 and grew to be one of the world's greatest automotive successes. The achievement was due to a combination of good products and a well-crafted image. Over the years, legions of Chevrolet dealers served on the front lines, riding the crests and surviving the falls the turbulent twentieth century handed them.

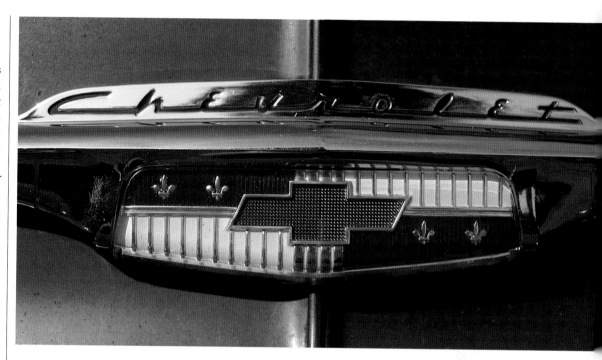

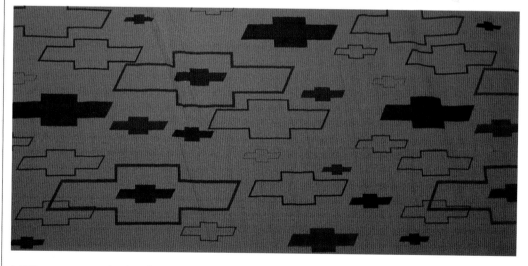

A 1961 announcement-day shroud. From the Tom Meleo collection.

7

Culberson-Stowers collection

This is not a history book. This is a collection. Chevrolet dealerships number in the thousands today, and many thousands have come and gone. Many of their stories have gone and will go unheard, but several longstanding Chevrolet dealerships shared their stories for this book, and many more opened their photo archives. Dedicated Chevrolet memorabilia collectors furnished some of America's finest commercial art—from the catchy, kitschy sales literature to the historically profound service bulletins, manuals, and legal documents.

The Chevrolet dealerships and dealers in these pages represent the thousands that enabled Chevrolet to have such a profound impact on America. When automobile enthusiasts pass a Chevrolet dealership, many can't help but pull over and invite themselves in to meet the family, see the old pictures on the walls, and seek out the gritty, street-level history. Whether it's a big, glamorous urban monument with sweeping architecture and acres of glass windows or a small-town family business with a 100-year-old

Culberson-Stowers collection

From the Tom Meleo collection.

From the Tom Meleo collection.

storefront that began its life selling cars in front of a dirt street, a Chevrolet dealership always has a special draw.

The dealers are just as much a part of Chevrolet's heritage as the dealerships. Some worked from plush offices with leather chairs and opulent décor, while others set their tools down, wiped the grease off their hands, and assumed the role of a salesperson when customers walked into the showroom. They each had the factory behind them, along with all its virtues and faults, good and bad decisions, and solid, but not always perfect, products. They also had the public in front of them, with all its honesty and fickleness, needs and demands, and reason and madness. And they had American history below them, with its freedom and regulation, inspiration and discouragement, and riches and poverty. Through it all, they always had that Bowtie above them.

This book showcases only a small sampling of those who have served as Chevrolet dealers, and one can only imagine the stories that have disappeared with time. Still, this book attempts to capture the remaining tales and, in doing so, hopes to offer a glimpse into an important part of twentieth-century history.

Many issues came between Louis Chevrolet and William Durant. One of their biggest disagreements stemmed from Durant's insistence on building low-priced cars as competition with Ford. Chevrolet wanted to build high-quality, well-engineered luxury cars. This difference of opinion came to a head in 1913 when Chevrolet stormed out of Durant's office. However, five years later, Durant introduced a car that would have made Chevrolet proud—if only he'd been able to stand Durant's behavior long enough to see the idea come to fruition. The Model Ds were large, comfortable touring cars and roadsters with smooth, quiet, 55-horsepower, overhead-valve V-8s. The distinctive models managed to have an accessible $1,500 price tag. This excellent example resides in Tom Meleo's collection.

PART I

The Chevrolet Business

Many historians consider 1896 to be the American automobile industry's formative year. It was that year that the Duryea brothers built about a dozen "motor-wagons" specifically for sale to the public, launching the explosion that would take the American auto industry from the nineteenth century into the twenty-first.

Thousands of company names came and went—Milburn, Cameron, Autocar, McFarlan, K.R.I.T, Marion, King, Frontenac. Some of the companies produced fine, quality cars, while others produced quirky, experimental cars with six and eight wheels, gunpowder-fueled engines, phone booth–shaped bodies, and heated steering wheels. Some companies were headed by visionary, though sometimes misguided, geniuses. Others existed in name only. Bogus stock certificates lured excited investors into betting their futures on companies that hung elaborate signs on empty buildings and disappeared into the night with millions of dollars.

In the first decade or so of the twentieth century, debate revolved around which type of fuel should propel these new automobiles. At the time, it was easier to find a place to get an electric car's batteries charged than it was to find a place to buy gasoline or kerosene. Detroit Electric, Fritchle, and Ohio Electric were betting the electric cell would remain the dominant source of energy. But with Stanley Steam setting land speed records of well over 100 miles per hour by 1906 and the public's desire to venture further beyond the range of a single battery charge, the fuel-burning automobile left the electric car in the dust.

Locomobile began its 30-year life in 1899. It was one of the industry's stars and one of the first to start thinking about making cars attractive. Using bodies designed by Tiffany and interiors devised by the leading decorators of the time, Locomobile foreshadowed the automotive design houses to come.

Manufacturing techniques advanced quickly, and Henry Ford received the majority of credit for perfecting the assembly line. Ford's production process brought inexpensive transportation to the masses in 1909 in the form of the Model T.

GENERAL MOTORS

William Durant and Benjamin Briscoe had the same idea at about the same time. The exact date is hard to pin down, but around 1905, each decided there were too many independent automobile companies. They believed the industry would be better off if the numerous companies were consolidated into a few large conglomerates. The race was on.

Some argue that Briscoe took the first steps in that race by forming the United States Motor Company. Briscoe had made a small fortune in the sheet-metal industry by 1900 and had owned the Buick Motor Company. He had experienced great success in the automobile business with Jonathan Maxwell, formerly of Oldsmobile, building the technologically sophisticated Maxwell car.

Durant picked up Buick in 1904, having already made his fortune with the Durant-Dort

Carriage Company. Within a year, Durant presided over a 2,000 percent increase in the value of Buick stock. Conflicting magazine articles from the 1930s allege there was a meeting in 1906 among William Durant, Jonathan Maxwell, Henry Ford, and Ransom Olds discussing the possibility of merging into a single supercompany. While this meeting did not result in a conglomerate, Durant's performance with Buick gave him the confidence to form General Motors in 1908.

The competition between Briscoe's United States Motor Company and Durant's General Motors was fierce, with each buying up every car company it could afford. On the strength of Maxwell, Briscoe bought Stoddard-Dayton, Columbia, Brush, and several others. Durant's massive Buick profits allowed him to acquire Oldsmobile, Cadillac, and other small car companies. Both Briscoe and Durant bought up various venders, companies supplying materials to the auto industry.

Briscoe and Durant were brilliant businessmen. Both had been enormously successful, but the competition between General Motors and the United States Motor Company was not wisely administered on either man's part. Durant and Briscoe ran the race on hubris, and they both lost.

By 1910, General Motors was financially strained to the breaking point, and a group of bankers took over the company and showed William Durant to the door.

William Durant was determined to get General Motors back, but he needed a lot of money and a hook. What he was missing was a powerful name to bet his future on, a name that would sell cars. In 1907, Buick formed a racing team with a trio of French immigrant brothers, siblings who were already known for racking up inventions in Europe including pumps for the wine industry and high-tech racing bicycles. While all were above-average race drivers, one of the brothers, Arthur, became Durant's personal chauffeur, and another, Gaston, held various positions that contributed to the race team. In 1909, the Buick racing team won 90 percent of the races it entered. The star of the team, the

Swiss

Culberson-Stowers collection

brother the public came to know and root for, was in the driver's seat of Buick's first successful racing cars. His name was Louis.

CHEVROLET

Chevrolet was incorporated in November 1911, and the new automobile debuted for the 1912 season. The Classic Six was a large, attractive, high-quality car with a dark blue body, black fenders and hood, and dark gray wheels. Priced at over $2,200, it gave the buyer many standard features including a self-starter, speedometer, electric headlights, electric dash light, accessory spare wheel carriers, 20-gallon fuel tank with gas gauge and two-gallon auxiliary tank, and running board–mounted tool kit. The chassis met the standards of the time with dual springs in front and a worm-and-sector steering gear modern enough to serve the auto industry in various forms into the 1930s.

William Durant was back on his feet by 1913, and Chevrolets were rolling out of the plant. The Classic Six returned with two economy lines alongside—the Light Six, the four-cylinder Royal Mail roadster, and the Baby Grand touring car. Automobiles were quickly overcoming their crude beginnings, and Chevrolets were very appealing, up-to-date cars. Sales totals for 1913 reached 5,005 cars, up from 2,999 in 1912. Chevrolet bought more plant space from Maxwell in Tarrytown, New York; the company established a West Coast sales office in Oakland, California; and the stage was set for Chevrolet dealerships.

Reportedly, most people liked Durant until they went into business with him. Those who worked with him discovered the insistent, hard-driven, absolutist executive with an overreaching gambler's streak. In the midst of all the success of the 1913 season, tensions grew

between William Durant and Louis Chevrolet. Durant wanted to build inexpensive economy cars to compete with Ford's Model T, and Chevrolet wanted the car that bore his name to be a luxurious, high-quality, well-engineered vehicle. Neither man would budge. Eventually, Chevrolet walked out, realizing only later that he had left his own name behind under Durant's ownership, just as David Buick and Ransom Olds had done.

Durant had conceived Chevrolet as a means to get General Motors, or GM, back, and it worked. Chevrolet profits were high, and Durant bought up GM stock until he regained controlling interest in the fall of 1915. Durant's habits were back as well, and by 1920, Durant was out once more, never to be associated with General Motors again. In that five years, however, Durant created a permanent marque.

The Model 490, named for its retail price, appeared in 1916 and went head-to-head with the Model T. It was a larger, sturdier, more comfortable, more attractive, and more technologically advanced alternative to Henry's Flivver. On the other end of the spectrum, one of Louis Chevrolet's dreams came true in his absence when Chevrolet built its first V-8 model late in 1917. The Model D was offered as a large, comfortable touring car, or roadster, complete with a smooth, quiet, 55-horsepower, overhead-valve V-8 that looked 30 years newer than it actually was. Its sweeping body lines were trimmed with beautiful wood that ran along the tops of the doors and rose and curved gently over the dashboard, eventually meeting the windshield frame, which was also trimmed in wood. With all these features, this distinctive model still managed to

continued on page 17

The cars that launched Chevrolet's success. The Classic Six heavyweight evolved from William Durant's efforts with Republic and Little. It gave way to the Light Four Model H. The Model H offered Chevrolet its first mass success with the Royal Mail roadster and Baby Grand touring car, which were unveiled for the 1913 and 1914 seasons. From the Tom Meleo collection.

1953 Direct Dealer Selling Agreement

What It Took to Be a Chevrolet Dealer

The contract's simplicity is amazing. The 20-page agreement defines the parties and lays out what their responsibilities will be. It includes a three-page set of signatures, the "Dealer Statement of Ownership, Financial Interests, and Active Management," and the "Policies on Dealer Adjustments."

The agreement defined Chevrolet as the "Seller," the dealership as the "Dealer," and the customer as the "Purchaser." Once the Purchaser bought the car, he or she became an "Owner."

The agreement granted the Dealer the right to sell Chevrolet products and use the Chevrolet name in all promotion. Then the contract turned its attention immediately to what the Seller and Dealer would do for each other. The agreement required the Dealer to provide the Seller with a "Ten-Day Report." Every ten days, the Dealer would provide the factory with a report of sales for the last, presumably, two weeks. Every month, the Dealer would have to provide the factory with a sales estimate for the next three months. The agreement explained that these two provisions would help the factory plan its upcoming production.

Classic car buffs and dealers fondly remember announcement days every fall when the searchlights came on, the curtains were drawn from the dealership windows, and the exciting new models were unveiled. Things were a little more complicated than they appeared to the public. In the midst of the party, last year's models were usually still sitting around, not yet sold. In certain years, such as 1949, 1955, 1959, 1961, and 1965, the previous year's Chevrolets were immediately

disregarded as old-fashioned. Luckily, when such cases arose, the agreement provided an allowance to the Dealer from the Seller. For every vehicle from the previous year still in the Dealer's stock, the Seller would pay the Dealer 4 percent of the car's average list price. The agreement excluded individual cars that the Dealer had used as demonstrators. Chevrolet also made it clear that if new features were brought out on new models, Chevrolet was under no obligation to modify the features of the new model onto the old models in the Dealer's stock.

The agreement also granted the Dealer the right to sell "Genuine Chevrolet parts and accessories." This written statement made car enthusiasts wonder if the contract's wording was the inspiration for the company's successful Genuine Chevrolet advertising campaign of the 1990s. The agreement made it very clear that it did not grant the Dealer the right to act as Chevrolet's agent or legal representative.

The agreement's "Operating Requirements" called upon the Dealer to "maintain a place of business including a salesroom, service station, parts and accessories facilities, and used-car facilities satisfactory to the Seller and to maintain the business hours customary in the trade." The contract also granted Chevrolet the right to inspect the dealership and required the Dealer to submit written notice of any changes to the property or changes in location, including the addition of used-car lots.

Under the heading "Building Service for Dealer," Chevrolet offered a useful service. It stated that the "Seller will, upon request, but without liability to Dealer with respect thereto, furnish to Dealer a suggested building plan and

layout, but such plan and layout will not be intended for use as a complete working plan and will be furnished solely as a suggestion." These plans may have played a factor in the sweeping, neon, artsy style of dealership design that automotive history buffs admire today.

Later in the document, the agreement required the Dealer to conform to the Seller's uniform accounting system and allowed the Seller routine examination of the Dealer's records.

Shortly thereafter, the agreement shifts gears and advises the Dealers how to handle the public. The document explains procedures for selling vehicles, maintaining a sales staff, maintaining sales and service records, and investigating and handling customer complaints. After the automobile drought of World War II, the car-hungry public filled dealers' waiting list. The resulting bribery, trickery, and black-marketeering on the part of some dishonest dealers and customers was a black eye to the many honest dealers. Words to this effect surely existed on prewar agreements, but in 1953, with the memories of these frauds still fresh, the "Treatment of Purchasers" was heavily relied on. It said that the "Dealer recognizes the importance of free competition, of selling Chevrolet products at fair prices with relation to his costs, of satisfactory treatment of purchasers, and the necessity of preventing any unfair or deceptive actors or practices in the sale of Chevrolet motor vehicles in order to protect the Chevrolet name and trademarks and protect and promote the goodwill of Seller attached thereto."

Highlights of the "Treatment of Purchasers" include:

A. Informing Purchasers as to the Details of Their Purchases: Dealer will advertise his delivered prices in this town and will inform retail purchasers of such prices and will give them itemized invoices covering the details of their purchases.

B. Representations as to the Contents of Charges: Dealer will not make any misleading statements or misrepresentations as to the items making up his total selling price or as to the prices related to such items not make any statements intended to lead any purchaser to believe that a greater portion of the selling price of a new Chevrolet motor vehicle or chassis represents transportation charges and Factory Handling Charges than the amounts of such items actually charged and paid for by Dealer.

C. Right of Retail Purchaser to Buy a New Car Without Purchasing Optional Equipment or Accessories: Dealer recognizes that a retail customer has the right to purchase new Chevrolet motor vehicles without being required to purchase any optional equipment of accessories as Dealer, therefore, will either remove any optional equipment or accessories which the purchaser does not want.

The agreement also detailed what happened once a Purchaser became an Owner. The "Care of Owner" section required the Dealer to deliver the car to the customer in operable condition, perform the necessary maintenance to honor the customer's warranty, keep the service department stocked with commonly needed parts, use only Chevrolet parts, and have on hand the special tools required to work on Chevrolet vehicles.

In 1953, Chevrolet's warranty period was 90 days or 4,000 miles from the date of delivery to the Owner. A special policy covered the vehicle for 12 months or 12,000 miles.

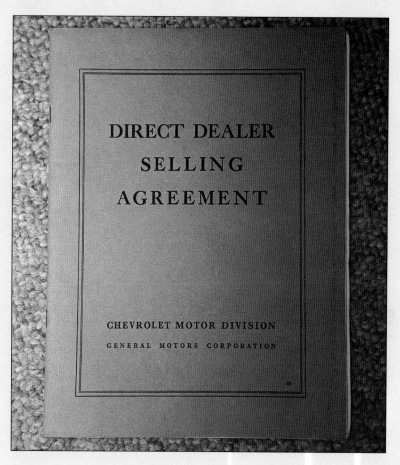

Brad Bowling

Some easily damaged items were only covered for the 90-day warranty period. These items included paint, trim fabric, upholstery, seats, spark plugs, oil filters, headlights, light bulbs, radio tubes, radio vibrators, seat covers, and clocks. Batteries and tires were covered by their individual manufacturers' warranties.

Dealers were reimbursed an allowance for warranty repairs. During the warranty period, the dealers received 65 percent of the cost of their labor charges, and parts were sold at cost plus 10 percent.

For decades, dealers of all brands have dealt with dreaded sign requirements such as, "Dealer will purchase, erect, and maintain at his expense the following signs: A. Product Sign B. Service Sign C. Other Necessary Signs." All automotive brands have required their dealers to erect new signs to keep up with changing fashions. Unfortunately, these signs come with a high price, and often, dealers have to take out lengthy loans to pay for them.

The agreement also explained the plan of action if the Dealer terminated the contract. It detailed everything from the termination of orders and deliveries to the handling of transactions after termination. It discussed how Sellers could repurchase merchandise from Dealers, and how to deal with real property that was owned, partially owned, or partially leased. The Direct Dealer Selling Agreement may not be as simple or personal as a handshake, but in the business of automobiles, it's the next best thing.

Chevrolet narrowed its sites on Ford country—the low-priced consumer market in which Henry's Model T dominated. Although the Ford was extremely successful, it stopped evolving substantively around 1915, just as Chevrolet brought out its direct competitor to the Model T. Chevrolet's 490 was named for its selling price and offered a more technologically advanced package. As the auto industry settled into norms in the 1920s, Chevrolet's 490 met those norms better than Ford. It showcased a floor-mounted, three-speed transmission that seemed more conventional than Ford's three-pedal planetary system. The Chevrolet gave the driver and passengers more room, higher body quality, and better-sprung suspension. From the Tom Meleo collection.

continued from page 13

have an accessible $1,500 price tag. The Model D was only built for a couple of years, but Louis Chevrolet would have been proud if only Durant hadn't driven him from the company.

Durant's second and permanent ouster from General Motors coincided with the fading of the auto industry's maverick days. As the 1920s rolled in, car companies settled into calmer, more professional corporate norms. Gone were the executive dictators with their ingenious creativity and notorious temperaments. The industry would never again be as exciting or free to create, but it would be more stable, honest, and reliable.

William Durant died in 1947 at the age of 72. At the time of his death, he was the manager of a bowling alley with some interest in a grocery store on the side. In 1938, Louis Chevrolet took medical retirement from his job as a General Motors assembly line mechanic. He died in 1941.

The Model Ds were large, comfortable touring cars and roadsters with smooth, quiet, 55-horsepower, overhead-valve V-8s. The distinctive models managed to have an accessible $1,500 price tag. This excellent example resides in Tom Meleo's collection.

Advance Design Trucks, 1947–1954

One Small Step for Chevrolet, One Giant Leap for Truck-kind

by James Hinckley

The Advance Design Chevrolet truck was born on June 28, 1947, and it was everything the name implied. Gone was the side-opening hood. It was replaced with a modern, front-opening hood for easier access to the engine compartment. The headlights were swallowed by growing front fenders, and the lights' lower, wider gaze lit the road better than the 1946 models. Door hinges were concealed for smoother body lines.

As innovative and exciting as the new styling was, the redesigned cab represented the biggest change and provided drivers with, for the first time in a truck, an interior engineered for increased comfort, aesthetic appeal, and safety. The cab interior had grown to provide an additional 8 inches of hip room and 3-1/2 inches at the shoulder. The seat was well

An Advance Design pickup is still used daily in William L. Morris Chevrolet's adjoining citrus orchards.

The Advance Design trucks were a boon to Chevrolet dealerships, and a sales guide listed key points to be included in every presentation.

1. The doors close easier and more solidly without slamming, remain closed until opened, require only a gentle push or pull to open and stay open due to a catch mechanism.

2. A larger steering wheel, coupled with new steering geometry, make for easier steering and more positive control.

3. A radio, designed specifically for the rigorous demand placed on trucks, available as an option.

4. Both doors lock easily from the inside by a mechanism operated by the door handle.

5. Storage room available under the seat for tools.

Bill Morris shows a Chevrolet Truck Data Book that salesmen carried to help explain their trucks' virtues to customers. This example features Chevrolet's late 1950s Task Force series trucks.

crafted, with 35 extra coil springs for better support. Seat tracking was also new in this series and allowed for the seat to rise along an inclined plane as it moved forward to provide more comfortable driver positioning and improved visibility.

The fixed, two-piece windshield was taller than in previous models, and this increased visibility enhanced the overall modern appearance of the truck. The optional rounded rear-quarter glasses also added to the truck's good looks and resulted in a 40 percent increase in total cab window space over the 1946 models.

6. One key fits all locks—ignition, passenger door, and dispatch box.

7. Instruments are now grouped in two large dials directly ahead of the driver with larger figures that are easier to read.

8. Foot pedals and the gearshift lever repositioned for more convenient operation.

The Advance Design series represented a quantum leap in truck design and was the result of extensive interviews with truck owners and dealers. The nationwide survey indicated that the appearance of trucks, especially among fleet operators, was becoming more important, but truck buyers were not willing to sacrifice endurance, utility, or economy of operation in the name of sporty looks. The survey also revealed that operators wanted roomier cabs with more comfort features. Visibility was also a major concern. The success

of the Advance Design series trucks leaves little doubt that Chevrolet listened and acted.

The cornerstone of the company's success, however, was still the dealer. Even though the new Chevrolet trucks represented many firsts for utilitarian vehicles, they were still just trucks. More than ten years later, the truck still had not progressed much in the eyes of the consumer.

If a dealer wanted to sell trucks, he had to know the customers and their special needs. If the market warranted it, the dealer might even expand to include a truck center that specialized in the unique needs of the truck buyer.

Bud Webster of Webster Motors in Cody, Wyoming, became quite adept at understanding the market needs in his area—two-speed, rear-axle trucks for the beet farmers; two-speed rear axles and "brownie" auxiliary gearboxes for the oil companies—and truck sales soon represented a full 20 percent of his business. Other dealerships achieved similar success simply by getting to know the workers in the community—the roofers, miners, farmers, carpenters, contractors, plumbers—and providing service before, during, and after the sale as well as catering to their special needs.

With extensive and intimate knowledge of his market in Kingman, Arizona, Roy Dunton of Dunton Motors was able to acquire the contract to supply Mohave County trucks within months after he acquired a Chevrolet franchise. This was soon followed by a deal to provide trucks for a large mining operation in the mountains north of Kingman.

In 1950, dealerships received an additional boost to meet the special needs of their customers. That year marked the introduction of NAPCO four-wheel-drive conversions for any Chevrolet or GMC truck. The NAPCO conversion consisted of a two-speed transfer case with ratios of 1:1 and 1.941:1 and a special front differential that was actually a modified Chevrolet/GMC rear differential.

The kit was not a factory-installed option, so the customer had to purchase a new Chevrolet or GMC truck and special order the NAPCO package. The modification would actually be completed at

Showroom banners in Tom Meleo's collection tout the qualities of the Advance Design Chevrolet trucks to the legions of customers who lined up for them.

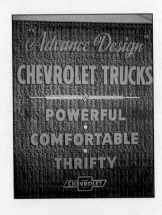

a NAPCO plant in Minneapolis or Detroit or at a NAPCO distributor—quite often a Chevrolet dealership. For the dealership that installed the components, there was the possibility of added profit because the stock front axle and drive shaft could be sold to the customer with the promise that when the truck was traded in, the NAPCO kit could be transferred to the new truck.

With the introduction of the NAPCO option, Chevrolet dealers could finally target the truck market, which, up until then, was almost entirely dominated by Dodge and Jeep. Sales were now limited only by a dealer's lack of imagination or inability to be aggressive.

For the vehicular world, the Advance Design trucks represent a milestone in truck development and marketing. For Chevrolet dealerships, they sparked a dominance of the light truck market that would last for more than 20 years.

Ferman Chevrolet's massive Truck Center basking in the Tampa, Florida, sun in the early 1960s. Ferman Chevrolet had just made a fleet sale of new trucks to a Clark forklift dealership. *Ferman Chevrolet collection*

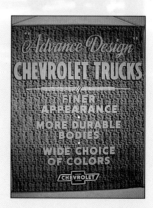

21

Culberson-Stowers collection

PART II

The Cars and the Modern Era

The 490 entered the 1920s as Chevrolet's "bread and butter," establishing the marque as GM's low-priced offering. But GM still had technological advancements in mind for this price range. In 1923, the 490 was replaced by the smoother-bodied Model F, dubbed "the Superior." Looking very much like the Superior, the Copper-Cooled Chevrolet was the car that could have symbolized the entire industry's next step forward. Franklin was the company most credited with air-cooled engine technology in the first half of the twentieth century, but Franklins were expensive, and Chevrolet wanted to produce an air-cooled car in the economy class. In 1918 and 1919, William Durant became interested in the work of Charles Kettering. Kettering's credits include efforts toward the self-starter, high-voltage ignition systems, high-compression engines, Freon refrigerant, and a two-cycle diesel engine.

Air-cooled engines were expensive to produce because the iron cooling fins on the cylinder head and engine block had to be either welded on or cast into the components. Kettering had come up with the technology to cheaply produce air-cooled engines by folding and pleating sheets of copper into finned plates and attaching them to the engine block by baking them in a 1,400-degree oven he designed. Pierre DuPont took over as head of General Motors in 1920, and K. W. Zimmersheid was appointed general manager of Chevrolet. Both were enthused with the air-cooled engine concept and gave Kettering the green light. DuPont was so sure the four-cylinder Copper-Cooled engine would work for Chevrolet that he began initiating a plan to convert the entire Oldsmobile line to air-cooled six-cylinder engines.

The Copper-Cooled Chevrolet was, in short, a disaster. Behind the louvered grille, a squirrel cage–style fan driven by a wide belt from the crankshaft forced air through a system of shrouds and over the copper cooling fins. The shrouding didn't allow enough airflow to evenly cool the engine, which may have contributed to the engine's incurable preignition problem. In addition to causing annoying, audible knocking, continuous preignition can burn valves and melt pistons, and the Copper-Cooled Chevrolets preignited badly at moderate speeds in 60- to 70-degree air temperatures. According to some automotive historians, the Copper-Cooled Chevrolet was the American auto industry's first recall. Production was halted at 759 cars, and only about 100 Copper-Cooled Chevrolets were sold of the 500 or so shipped to dealerships. About 150 of them were given to GM representatives. Over 200 were scrapped while still in the factory.

Alfred P. Sloan replaced DuPont in the spring of 1923 and quickly discontinued the Copper-Cooled Chevrolet and halted all development on the air-cooled Oldsmobile. Some believe the whole Copper-Cooled affair may have contributed to Zimmersheid's nervous breakdown. Kettering may have initiated the catastrophe, but he was also the author of the storm's silver lining when he worked out a formula for a better fuel for the Copper-Cooled Chevrolet and other cars with preignition problems. For the next 70 years, his formula, called "leaded gasoline," was used by millions of motorists.

THE BOWTIE RISES

The modern era swept Chevrolet quickly, and the 1925 through 1928 models were progressively more refined in appearance and appointments. Plus, they didn't cost much more than Ford's Model T, a car that was still locked in 1915 technology. Chevrolet's Achilles' heel, however, was its cone clutch—a shallow, cone-shaped device with leather surfaces exposed to the elements in the absence of any kind of bell housing. Adjustments were the bane of dealership service departments that constantly had to undo the work of shade-tree mechanics who commonly replaced the clutch's adjustable ridges with pieces of broken hacksaw blades. Longtime Atlanta, Georgia, Chevrolet dealer Hal Smith began his career in the service department of his father's Chevrolet dealership and claims that the company's replacement of the cone clutch with a modern disc clutch in 1925 literally saved Chevrolet.

Smith says the disc clutch was even more important to Chevrolet than the six-cylinder engine in 1929, but the 194-ci, overhead-valve six was far more important to the public's imagination. Its basic design would serve Chevrolet and, occasionally, other GM divisions for the next 50 years. Guys talking about cars over coffee still call it the "Stovebolt Six." Some say that's because of the head bolt design, while others say it's in honor of the cast-iron pistons that the engine used much longer than it should have. Regardless, the car kept with technological advancements that were rapidly sweeping the industry. Ten years before, Hudson had perfected balanced crankshafts, and Dodge had made

Above: Chevrolet's cone clutch, which finally went away in 1925, had been a thorn in the paw for dealership service departments. "It had the reputation for holding the record for the broad jump!" says Hal Smith, longtime Chevrolet dealer of Atlanta, Georgia. "It was almost impossible to let the clutch out easily so the car wouldn't jump…. I remember working in the shop and replacing all those rear ends because the cone clutch had jerked them loose. The disc clutch made it possible to move that car into a sales position to where it would sell. The six-cylinder engine [in 1929] was a good thing. They came out with the overhead valves, and it was a remarkably good motor and a remarkable car, but really, it was the disc clutch that saved the day."

great strides in the areas of engine oiling and cooling. Advancements of this nature quickly filtered down to the economy-car price range. Chevrolet's sixes were more durable, were easily repaired, and made life in the showrooms and service departments much better for the dealers.

By 1929, C. S. Mott was the head of General Motors. While visiting Buffalo, New York, he attended a fundraising rally for the YMCA. The speaker was a passionate, riveting young man named William Holler who had the crowd on its feet in thundering applause, burning to become boosters for the YMCA. Mott immediately hired Holler and put him in charge of Chevrolet sales. Mott could not have known he would change the course of history, not just for Chevrolet, but for the entire industry. Holler instituted the Quality Dealer Program, which imposed tightly enforced requirements on dealers to become leading members of their communities and to tirelessly serve their customers. In exchange for their efforts, Holler became the dealers' advocate and went to bat for them

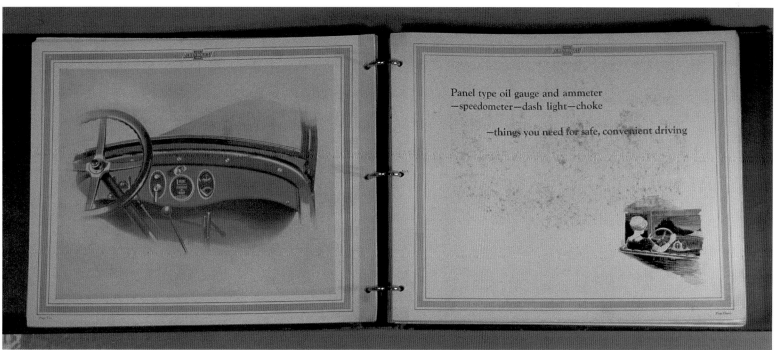

Chevrolet sales literature from the 1920s. From the Tom Meleo collection.

25

against market forces, the competition, GM's decision makers, and the Great Depression, which crashed down just as Holler was hired. Chevrolet dealers served their communities as no other dealers did and cemented customer loyalty that Chevrolet may still be measurably enjoying in the twenty-first century.

With unemployment skyrocketing, bread lines lengthening, and banks closing, buying a new car was the last thing most Americans planned to do. But Chevrolet, under pressure from Holler, created a car so attractive that it is still considered a prize among collectors. The 1932 Chevrolets looked like miniature Duesenburgs and were, without a doubt, the prettiest economy cars up to that time. Their proportions made them look longer, lower, and wider than they actually were, and their chromed hood-vent doors and gracefully curving headlight standards set their styling against far more expensive cars. Unfortunately, the 1932s hid another story under their skins. The beautiful new Chevrolets were plagued with serious

Chevrolet promotional offerings from the 1920s. This catalog, from Tom Meleo's collection, includes various styles of outdoor signs and streetcar advertisement placards for the urban dealer.

The wise old owl offers his advice for 1929. From the Tom Meleo collection.

problems—exceptionally poor fuel economy, weak axles, outdated straight-gear transmissions, and an unreliable and somewhat dangerous free-wheeling option. Longtime St. Louis–area Chevrolet dealer Jim Meagher got his start working in a Chevrolet dealership's service department and later went on to a career as regional parts manager for the Midwest before taking on his own dealership. Meagher remembers a big difference between early and late 1932 models, with the later examples having had nearly all their ills cured and having reliability to match their looks.

WEAK IN THE KNEES, BUT STANDING STRONG

In 1934, Chevrolet made a technological leap with independent front suspension. Knee-Action

rode softer, handled better, and made driving an economy car much more pleasant. But the Knee-Action units were large, cumbersome blocks of machinery bolted to the frame preceding each front wheel, and the early examples created some problems for the dealerships. By comparison, Plymouth's 1934 independent front suspension is still found on cars and trucks in the twenty-first century. Plymouth's independent suspension may have been better than Chevrolet's, but it only lasted one year due to production costs, and Chrysler would not apply independent front suspension to Dodges and Plymouths again until 1939.

Meanwhile, Chevrolet continued to offer Knee-Action through 1938, with most of the problems ironed out by the last couple of years of the system's run. Some dealers describe Knee-Action as having ridden too soft, making the little cars a bit hard to control on bad roads. Still, Knee-Action was a great tool for getting customers into the showroom. Dealers were provided with Jounce Meters—large, brass, clock-like mechanisms that counted the bounces a car made over a measured course. The salesman strapped the Jounce Meter to the hood of a customer's old car, and the meter counted the bounces. Then he strapped it to the hood of a new Knee-Action Chevrolet and proved to the customer that, over the same course, the Chevrolet bounced less. He would even cite the medical advantages of Knee-Action.

The Knee-Action era saw Chevrolet improve in areas of body quality, comfort, and safety with all-steel roofs, larger bodies, four-wheel hydraulic brakes, better insulation, and the Stovebolt Six increased to 216 cubic inches. However, not everything ran perfectly. There were problems with water pump shafts walking out the front of the pump, sending the fan into the radiator. The bell housings were not always machined perfectly, causing the strain on the

continued on page 32

Knee-Action smoothed out the miles as Chevrolet's first independent suspension in 1934. From the Tom Meleo collection.

A Year at a Glance: 1942 Sales Material

The Last Splash before the War

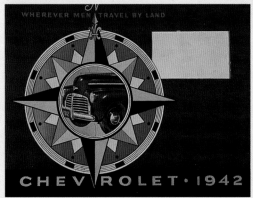

Decades before "interactive" was a popular term, both sections of the 1942 sales brochure had moving parts. When the flaps were pushed, pulled, or rotated as instructed, the pages were propelled into action. From the Tom Meleo collection.

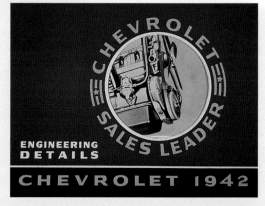

CHEVROLET . . . A CAR OF MANY CONCEALED VALUES

You can see the beauty of its exterior

You can feel the deep cushioned interior luxury

But . . . you must look underneath to learn the hidden values

GM's commercial artists gave dealers memorable imagery and an alluring richness of color, even for the corporation's least expensive make.

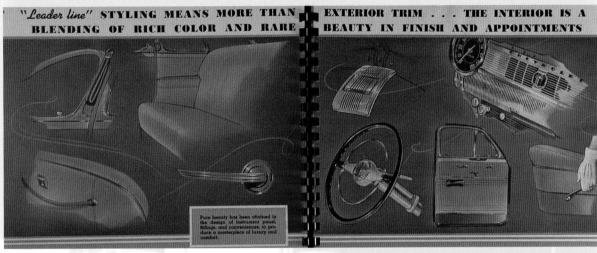

"Leader line" STYLING MEANS MORE THAN BLENDING OF RICH COLOR AND RARE EXTERIOR TRIM . . . THE INTERIOR IS A BEAUTY IN FINISH AND APPOINTMENTS

Pure beauty has been attained in the design of instrument panel, fittings, and conveniences, to produce a masterpiece of luxury and comfort.

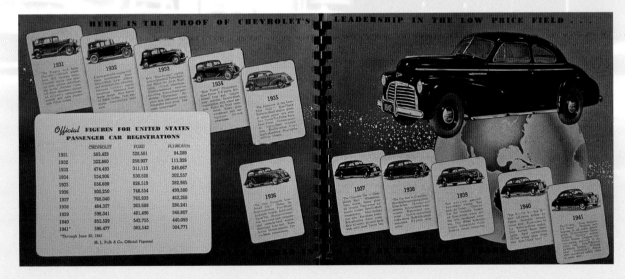

HERE IS THE PROOF OF CHEVROLET'S LEADERSHIP IN THE LOW PRICE FIELD . . .

Official FIGURES FOR UNITED STATES PASSENGER CAR REGISTRATIONS

	CHEVROLET	FORD	PLYMOUTH
1931	503,429	528,581	94,289
1932	322,860	258,927	111,926
1933	474,493	311,113	249,667
1934	534,906	530,528	302,557
1935	656,698	826,519	382,985
1936	930,250	748,554	499,580
1937	768,040	765,933	462,268
1938	464,337	363,688	286,241
1939	598,341	481,496	348,807
1940	853,529	542,755	440,093
1941*	596,477	382,542	304,771

*Through June 30, 1941

(R. L. Polk & Co. Official Figures)

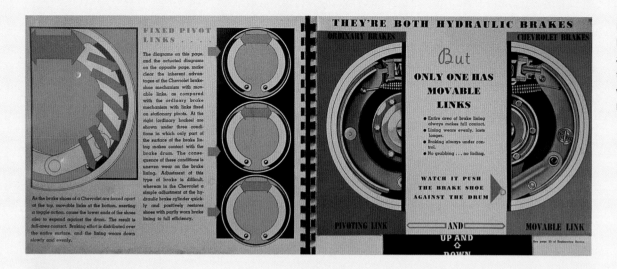

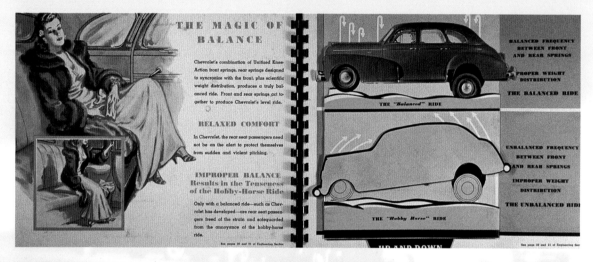

Brakes expand against their drums, bodies glide along while suspension absorbs the bumps, and engines rotate through complete cycles as the customer works Chevrolet's animated "Engineering Details" section of the book.

A brochure for 1942 features the charming drum major. The character was part of a recurring promotional theme well into the 1950s.

A giant, wall-mounted showroom album illustrated all the virtues of Chevrolet's Vacuum Shift for 1942. This page displays Chevrolet's smaller, more convenient shift pattern. From the Tom Meleo collection.

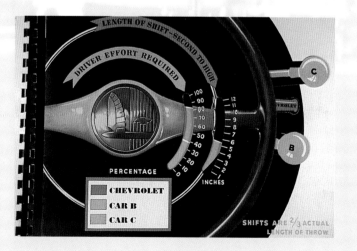

The Chevrolet sales force demonstrated how their cars made the driver work less to shift gears.

Chevrolet gave its dealers and customers the marque's first automatic transmission in 1950. Powerglide was an adaptation of Buick's Dynaflow. While the Dynaflow operated smoothly behind the big Roadmaster eights, it was considerably slower off the line with the smaller Buick eight found in the Supers. Behind the Chevrolet six, the Powerglide was downright slow. Still, with the Powerglide option, there was a much better rear-axle ratio that allowed small economy-class Chevrolets to run America's highways alongside the big cars.

Continued from page 29

transmission input shaft to eventually wear out the bearings or, in the worst cases, send the gears all over the street.

By 1940, Chevrolets were curvaceous, streamlined cars dripping with chrome. They hinted at what the future held. In the late 1930s, Chevrolet developed some of the most comfort-able seats in the economy-car class, a powerful feature for the salesman on a test drive.

MAKING A LIVING UNDER THE SMOKE OF WAR

By 1939, the smoke of war was drifting across the Atlantic, and the fallout of Germany's inva-sion of Poland soon reached the United States. For a nervous three years, dealers suspected they would be tightening their belts for war. Some dealers began stockpiling cars, parts, oil, tires, and dealership supplies, while others began selling off inventories, thinking the car business might come to a halt if war broke out.

When the Japanese bombed Pearl Harbor, there was a strange sense of relief. The uncer-tainty was over for car dealers, as well as the rest of the American population, and the crisis was

From the Tom Meleo collection.

after World War II were recycled 1942 models. Some competitors showed postwar innovations sooner than General Motors did, but they weren't necessarily more popular because of it. Studebaker's 1947 introduction of slab-sided bodies with fields of curving glass were mocked by consumers who asked, "Which way is it going?" Hudson's ultra-low-profile, step-down design for 1948 gave Jack Benny the opportunity to quip, "I fell down into my new Hudson and almost broke my neck."

There may have been laughter at Chevrolet dealerships, but it was probably nervous laughter. By 1948, Chevrolet's bulging bulk was looking very old-fashioned. Later in the 1948 model run, General Motors introduced new streamlined bodies for Cadillac and Olds. The new Olds 98 was appropriately called Futuramic, and dealers were happy to see the Chevrolet version of this new shape arrive in their showrooms in 1949 with flatter hoods, front fenders that didn't look bolted on, and curved windshields. The line of slick fastback bodies came under the name Fleetline.

Unfortunately, the new Fleetline bodies could not hide the fact that under the slick new sheet metal was a very old car with nearly every component in the drivetrain dating back to the early 1930s and some to the 1920s. Even by 1931, the 216-ci Stovebolt Six still didn't have pressurized oiling or insert bearings like Plymouth did. Driveshafts were still enclosed in a terribly awkward tube, along with a nagging little transmission leak inside it. This made clutches and universal joints very hard for service departments to work on. Rear-axle ratios were as low as 4.11, making the engines howl at speeds as low as 50 miles per hour in a country where freeways were inching their way into public consciousness. In spite of ungainly styling for 1949, Plymouths were more technologically advanced than Chevrolets in nearly every way. Fords had V-8s,

optional overdrive, and greatly improved suspension for 1949 and were certainly the most capable low-priced cars on the evolving freeways. The demure Nash 600 was capable of a consistent 25 to 30 miles per gallon as long as drivers weren't too demanding of power. Despite this competition, Chevrolet outsold them all, outpacing Plymouth alone five-to-one. William Holler had retired from Chevrolet in 1946, but the ghost of the Quality Dealer Program lingered, and loyal Chevrolet buyers would rather drive a Chevrolet with a 1929 drivetrain than a high-tech Plymouth or a fast, road-ready Ford.

conclusively defined. Dealers who had stockpiled supplies often provided items to dealers who had fewer resources. In addition to gasoline, car parts and tires were also rationed, and a robust black market bloomed. When the war ended in late 1945, dealerships had long waiting lists for new cars, and some became known for taking a little money on the side to move a person up the list. Members of the public sometimes bought new cars using questionable means and resold them for special payoffs. Those dealers who gained the reputation for participating in shady dealings didn't realize that the public has a long memory, and when postwar prosperity transferred the market from the sellers' hands to the buyers' hands, dealers of bad repute faded away.

As with most American car companies, Chevrolet's first three years' worth of offerings

From the Tom Meleo collection.

From the Tom Meleo collection.

CHEVROLET DEALERS GLIDE INTO POWER

Good things came to those who waited for technology to cross paths with the Chevrolet name. General Motors leapt forward with the introduction of the Hydra-Matic on Oldsmobiles in 1939. The modern, fully automatic transmissions were popular, but they went unmaintained through the war years and proved to need repairs far more often than the trouble-free manual transmissions that drivers had relied on for decades. It's possible that GM introduced the ultrasmooth Buick Dynaflow in 1948 to counter complaints from former Oldsmobile customers who didn't want another jerky transmission. Although equipped with an emergency "low" to provide engine braking while dropping down steep grades, Dynaflow did not actually shift gears, and all the ratio changes were accomplished with its modern torque converter.

By 1949, Pontiac had the Hydra-Matic, and Chevrolet was the only GM division lacking an automatic transmission. Chevrolet got its automatic in 1950 in the form of the Buick Dynaflow, rebadged as Powerglide. With its silent, mountain-moving, 323-ci straight-eight, a Dynaflow-equipped Buick Roadmaster could reach and effortlessly maintain very high cruising speeds. When optioned behind the considerably smaller eight of a Super, the Buick wasn't going anywhere too quickly and earned jeers of "Dynaflush" and worse. In spite of using the 235ci six found in GMC trucks and a Dynaflow hiding behind a different name, a Powerglide Chevrolet was just plain slow. Still, it had one pronounced virtue over a manual Chevrolet—a much better rear-axle ratio. The 4:11 rear end of a manual Chevrolet made the old-fashioned six howl at speeds as low as 45 to 50 miles per hour, but the approximately 15 percent lower rpm provided by the rear end found in Powerglide cars helped create Chevrolet's first true highway machines. Dealers may not have always recommended them for cities where Powerglide's leisurely accelerations and poor fuel economy could become tiresome, but in rural areas with a lot of paved highway between towns, Powerglide lived up to its name and glided effortlessly at 60 to 65 miles per hour. Dick Stowers of Culberson-Stowers Chevrolet in Pampa, Texas, enjoyed his first Powerglide on the flat, smooth 60 miles of U.S. Highway 60 between Pampa and Amarillo and recommended it without hesitation to customers living and driving in the same conditions.

For its third birthday, Powerglide received a valve body that made the transmission shift

Genuine Chevrolet replacement light bulbs from the 1930s. From the Tom Meleo collection.

between its former emergency low and drive gears. The following year, the new 1954 Chevrolets put the 235 in front of the Powerglide again—now with full-pressure engine oiling and insert bearings. Chevrolet was suddenly a modern car, but the best was yet to come.

THE SUPERHIGHWAYS CALL

The year 1953 marked the introduction of Chevrolet's first postwar "co-car," a completely different car produced simultaneously that also wore the Chevrolet name. The Corvette spoke of glamour, youth, and

continued on page 41

Left: In the late 1930s, when a customer decided to buy an optional clock or have one added to the car, the dealership service department pulled a glove box door off the shelf. From the Tom Meleo collection.

A Year at a Glance: 1954 Sales Material

The Last Splash before the Hot Ones

The Hot Ones of 1955 had not arrived yet, but the image of Chevrolet was definitely getting warmer. The 235ci six had filtered through all the division's offerings with insert bearings and pressurized oiling. Powerglide shifted on its own for the second year, and power brakes were available for the first time. Chevrolet technology was finally out of the 1920s, and GM's outstanding art department gave dealerships materials to prove it to the public. Elaborate wall hangings and explanatory brochures armed the salesmen with information on Chevrolet's new features. Examples of this can be found in the Keith Hill collection. *Brad Bowling*

Chevrolet's giant flip-chart-style showroom catalog tried to assure the people of America that their new purchase would take their family safely and economically down the rapidly expanding U.S. highways. This is from Keith Hill's collection. *Brad Bowling*

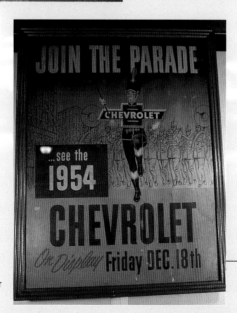

The cheerful drum major appears again for 1954. This is from Tom Meleo's collection.

In 1954, many of America's Chevrolet dealerships were still very small and had room for only three or four demonstrators. Fortunately, GM Photographic's Multi-Vu showed customers all of Chevrolet's available colors and body styles in 3-D. Most of Multi-Vu's images were culled from the same stock of photos as Chevrolet's postcards. This is from Keith Hill's collection. *Brad Bowling*

The 1954 Chevrolet upholstery selector resides in Keith Hill's collection. *Brad Bowling*

Announcement Day 1954. The search lights came on, the curtains came down, and the new Chevrolet was unveiled. Snacks and coffee were served with monogrammed utensils , and even the sugar-cube wrappers came with Bowtie logos on them. The lady of the house would go home with a bottle of Windsong perfume, and the children could busy themselves coloring scenes of Chevrolets from all the states. From the Keith Hill collection. *Brad Bowling*

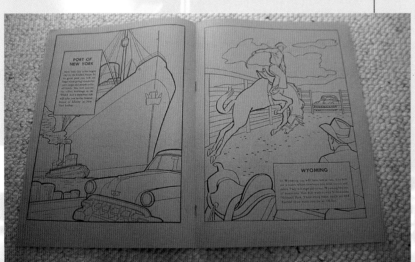

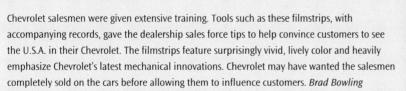

Chevrolet salesmen were given extensive training. Tools such as these filmstrips, with accompanying records, gave the dealership sales force tips to help convince customers to see the U.S.A. in their Chevrolet. The filmstrips feature surprisingly vivid, lively color and heavily emphasize Chevrolet's latest mechanical innovations. Chevrolet may have wanted the salesmen completely sold on the cars before allowing them to influence customers. *Brad Bowling*

In 1954, Chevrolet dealers could finally brag that their cars had full-pressure oiling and insert bearings on all their engines.

From the Tom Meleo collection.

Continued from page 35

highway-born freedom. The exquisite body was designed with input from famed General Motors stylist Henry Lauve. He claims some of the early Corvette's styling was inspired by sporty Fiats. Under the skin of the car was the standard Chevrolet six with some special modifications. The Corvette was given a V-8 in 1955 and progressed through the rest of the 1950s and clear into the next century. No other American car company regularly produced anything like the Corvette, but the model's production totals were never more than a few percent of Chevrolet's output. Other than certain dealers who took special interest in them, the Corvettes played almost no part in the day-to-day experience of most Chevrolet dealers.

THE HOT ONES

Veteran car dealers representing all makes of cars say they miss the exciting announcement days when the shades were pulled from the showroom windows and the new models were unveiled to a public whose curiosity had been teased through weeks of secrecy. Chevrolet dealers remember a 1955 announcement as one of their fondest. When the covers came off the "Hot Ones," the newly styled Chevrolets revealed beautiful two-tone paint schemes, colorful interiors with striking dashboards, and, under the hood, the best news of all—Chevrolet's first V-8 since 1919. The 265-ci V-8 came in a cast-iron package that would eventually serve as a General Motors standard clear past the turn of the century. This would propel the light, nimble Chevrolet with smooth acceleration never before associated with the marque. Gone was Chevrolet's image as solely a producer of economy cars.

If the 1955 Chevrolet looked a little unfinished, the 1956 update completed the package in true beauty, with a grille that looked finished, stylish taillights, and a handsome, two-tone paint scheme that was rivaled in beauty only by more expensive Dodges, DeSotos, and Mercurys.

Unfortunately, the party didn't last. Chevrolet dealers shook their heads at what they perceived as the backward step taken by the 1957 models. Although the small-block V-8 grew to the 283-ci that would serve it through the following decade and the car was available with an optional road-burning 348-ci big block and higher-tech Turboglide automatic transmission, the styling was a disaster. As the 1957 Chevrolet's badly updated 1955 styling sat in the showrooms, right across the street was a Ford dealership with all-new, mildly finned models that were wider, lower, longer, and just plain fresher cars.

If the 1957 Ford looked a few years newer than a 1957 Chevrolet, a 1957 Plymouth announced that the 1960s were coming, looking a decade newer than the Chevrolet. The Plymouth had rocket-shaped, space-age styling, compound curved glass, and hints of the following year's quad headlights. Most of all, both Fords and Plymouths were designed from the ground up with all their elements crafted to create a harmonized look even when they were sitting still. Chevrolets, on the other hand, were visually weighted down by an overly heavy front bumper theme that looked good only on big Oldsmobiles and by sharp, afterthought fins stuck to an otherwise pleasantly rounded body. Twenty-first-century collectors might not be aware that the 1957 Chevrolet's popularity only evolved after the cars were relegated to the used-car lots.

The 1958 Chevrolets provided dealers with badly needed styling updates, but Ford and Plymouth didn't need to update their styling from the previous year to still look newer than Chevrolet. The Bowtie caught up in a blistering hurry with its horizontally finned 1959 models, implementing cat-eye taillights, strangely slotted front ends, and heavy-handed dashboards. Despite the radical styling themes, the 1959 Chevrolet presented an unlikely cleanness, and the cars proved popular with the public, something that similar styling applied to Buick and Cadillac could not do in 1959.

continued on page 50

Jim Meagher—St. Charles, Missouri
The Occasional Lemon

Meagher helped solve some of Chevrolet's imperfections at the dealership level beginning in 1924.

The automobile's path has been long and rough. Chevrolet wasn't always able to avoid the potholes along the way. Jim Meagher told the tales of the unsung heroes hidden behind the glistening glass showrooms and flashing neon. He remembered what it was like to work far removed from the customers, back where the parts and service men perfected the Chevrolets that arrived at the dealerships a little less than perfect.

Jim Meagher gained some notoriety though the Midwest for putting together one of the finest collections of low-mileage Chevrolets anywhere in the world. His collection spanned the 1930s to the 1970s and included some models with only a few miles on their odometers. The collection was sold after a severe flood damaged his storage facilities in 1994. Meagher passed away in the mid-1990s, but he left behind 70 years' worth of memories.

In 1924, Meagher got a job pumping gas at a service station. The owner of Northside Chevrolet in St. Louis, Missouri, regularly bought gasoline at the station. When he

heard that young Jim wasn't going back to school after the Christmas break of 1924, he offered him a job in the parts department of his dealership.

In 1936, Meagher became a zone parts manager. His new job took him to Wichita,

Kansas; Detroit, Michigan; and Kansas City, Missouri, with a move or two back to St. Louis in between. After World War II, Meagher served on the faculty of Chevrolet's factory education program, training factory employees after they returned from the war. Meagher didn't want to

Jim Meagher (extreme left near chart) spent many years as a regional parts and service manager for Chevrolet. He identified and solved the problems the cars brought with them from the factory. Meagher began his career doing oil changes in a St. Louis dealership in the 1920s. By the mid-1950s, he owned his own dealership in St. Charles, Missouri. *Meagher family collection*

move anymore, so he bought an interest in the St. Charles Motor Company in St. Charles, Missouri—a city across the Missouri River from St. Louis. He became the sole owner of the enterprise in 1958 and named the business Jim Meagher Chevrolet-Oldsmobile.

The Copper-Cooled Chevrolet of 1923 was the company's first attempt at an air-cooled engine, but it was also the company's first failure and first major recall. In addition, the defeat triggered a nervous breakdown for the company's president. On the upside, the failure was the impetus behind Charles Kettering's experiments to add lead to gasoline. Kettering hoped to eliminate preignition and proved that failure really is sometimes the mother of invention.

Like Kettering, Meagher had a vested interest in seeing Chevrolet progress technologically, and his hands-on experience began immediately as he joined Northside Chevrolet.

"In the 1925–26 period, the casting on the starter where it bolted to the flywheel housing was a little troublesome," Jim Meagher remembered. "The Bendix spring would break, or the engine would kick back if the driver retarded the spark, and that would break the Bendix housing. That really wasn't a fault. It was just something that happened every once in a while. Also, in the 1920s and 1930s, the propeller shaft was inside a tube. You didn't have the open universal joints. There was a bushing in the back of the transmission that the propeller shaft rode in, and that bushing used to give us hell. It was oiled only by the transmission oil seeping back into it. There should have been a grease fitting on it, but there would have been no way to get at it.

In his later years, Meagher became a devotee of antique cars and eventually amassed a collection that included one Chevrolet for each year from 1926 to 1975. His 150-car collection included a large number of Oldsmobiles and Buicks with a few Nashes and Chryslers in the mix. Meagher family collection

The beautiful 1932 Chevrolet. Meagher report the earliest examples of this model year suffered from severe design and quality problems with a bad freewheeling device, extremely poor fuel economy, outdated transmissions, and fragile rear axles. The good news was that Chevrolet ironed out most of these problems by the end of the 1932 run. From the Tom Meleo collection.

"The 1934 models had the big Knee-Action units on both front wheels," Meagher continued. "They looked like big shock absorbers, and they were Chevrolet's first independent suspension. They had needle bearings in them [where the arms that supported the spindle pivoted in the unit during the up-and-down motion of the wheel]. The needle bearings were harder than the inner and outer surfaces they were rocking in, and they would dig in, making a washboard effect on the surfaces. We replaced hundreds of them.

Knee-Action, Chevrolet's first independent front suspension, was introduced in 1934. The unit was bolted to the frame, and the main body of the device contained the suspension spring. The large lever attached to the center of the hub and supported the weight of the car, and the small lever worked a lever-action shock absorber. Most of the Knee-Action's problems had been addressed by 1938, and the units became quite reliable. From the Tom Meleo collection.

The dealership I worked in was the only one in this area that had a front-end machine for aligning up the wheels. We were doing alignment work for practically the whole zone after their cars had been repaired. On the later Knee-Action units, the surfaces were hard enough, and they were all right."

According to Meagher, there were no serious problems through the late 1930s and up to World War II. He never mentioned the challenges Wyoming Chevrolet dealer Bud Webster encountered, such as Chevrolet's 1937 and 1938 water pump shafts working out of their housings and gouging the fans into the radiators. Meagher recalled that the public was not pleased with Chevrolet styling for 1939, and while many have been heard to criticize Chevrolet's vacuum shift, Meagher said the vacuum shift units were quite reliable and only encountered slight problems with the earliest examples. The way Meagher remembered it, serious difficulties didn't happen until the 1950s.

"We had problems with the early Powerglides [1950–52]. We had been very successful with the Hydra-Matic in the Oldsmobiles and Cadillacs, but the Powerglides were more of an adaptation of the Buick Dynaflow. They just didn't hold up. It seemed like all we were doing was transmission work until we got the later ones [in 1953] when they took the better aspects of both transmissions—the Hydra-Matic and the Dynaflow—and did the shifting with oil pressure. The truth of the matter is that our transmissions were really refinements of the planetary transmissions used by Henry Ford on the Model T, except that on the Model T, you did all the work with the foot pedal."

Chevrolet models from the late 1950s are much prized by collectors, but they are not without their bittersweet traits.

"On the early V-8s, the factory had been using extremely hard piston rings, and they were bad for using oil because the rings wouldn't seat. The people who were used to Chevrolet's not using oil raise[d] particular hell, so we replaced a lot of rings in those, but the people who kept those hard rings and didn't complain about them later came up with automobiles that were damn near perfect, because eventually, those hard rings seated. Once that happened, that engine would run forever! As popular as they were, the '58s came out with that Air Ride suspension, and that was a complete flop. It didn't last long, and Chevrolet brought out a kit to replace Air Ride [with regular suspension]."

Meagher remembered the radical styling of the 1959 Chevrolet automobiles:

"There were no problems with the '59 other than the shock of the fins running horizontally. I drove one of the first '59s I had to New York, and of course, in New York City, you can walk almost as fast as you can drive. People were walking alongside of me as I

"We had problems with the early Powerglides [1950–52]," Meagher remembers. "We had been very successful with the Hydra-Matic in the Oldsmobiles and Cadillacs, but the Powerglides were more of an adaptation of the Buick Dynaflow. They just didn't hold up. It seemed like all we were doing was transmission work until we got the later ones [in 1953] when they took the better aspects of both transmissions—the Hydra-Matic and the Dynaflow—and did the shifting with oil pressure." This 1950 Chevrolet is from the Tom Meleo collection.

drove, asking, 'What is it?!' I had to explain that it was the '59 Chevrolet."

Jim Meagher took a refreshingly philosophical view of the car business and its predicaments.

"I don't think there is any such thing as a lemon. Usually, there's just a little problem that hasn't been found. Ivory Soap advertised being 99.44 percent pure. If you apply that analogy to 20,000 parts on a car from the cotter pins on up, you could have 112 parts that need to be replaced, and you've got to remember, that car was built by the guy who lives next door. I don't care what the car is, there are going to be little problems."

Fingertip Facts for the 1955 Chevrolet

Some of dealerdom's finest artifacts are its sales tools—brochures, giant catalogs, training films, and postcards.

Today, automobile enthusiasts have read *ad nauseam* how Chevrolet revamped its image for the 1955 season by introducing its first V-8 since 1917, taking the marque from economy cars to the competitive Hot Ones. Ford and Plymouth did likewise in 1955—Ford with a larger car and a safety campaign, and Plymouth with an all-new body and a considerably more advanced V-8. But Chevrolet is the one that's remembered and sought after by collectors.

How did Chevrolet get so much attention amid all this swirl of legitimate competition? One minor player in this game was *Fingertip Facts for the 1955 Chevrolet*—a pocket-sized paperback that a salesman could pull out anytime a customer even hinted at looking at a Plymouth or Ford.

Reprinted by Motorbooks International in 1994, this book is an informative, entertaining, jet-age gem that drips of the 1950s. From page to page, it swings from the brilliant to the ridiculous, from the factual to the fantastic, and from providing information to slinging utter salesmanship.

Some of the book is devoted to giving the salesman at-a-glance answers to customers' questions about the competition. Beautiful hand-drawn illustrations were obviously designed to engage customers. The pages are full of dubious comments about the competition's virtues, but even these are enjoyable glimpses back in time.

FEATURES

The book is printed entirely in black and white, but the illustrations are gorgeous. It is GM at its most artistic. The Chevrolets are stretched in

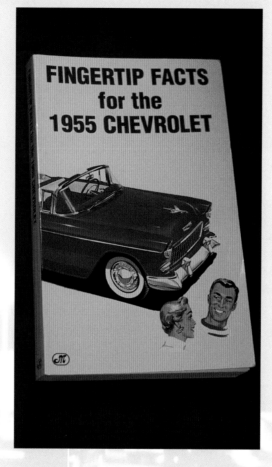

the hand-drawn illustrations, such as one picture of a model 150 four-door sedan. Lacking the side trim of a Bel Air, it was truly a short, stubby little car, but the artists stretched the car in all the illustrations.

The book counters the issue of short appearance by turning the reader's attention to a legitimate issue like Chevrolet's tighter turning radius. The Chevrolet can approach a steeper ramp than a Ford or a Plymouth without hooking a front or rear overhang.

In an attempt to prove that Chevrolet wasn't just selling image, one page features a beautiful illustration of the underside of the car, and another gives the customer great exploded views of the internal mechanics of the clutch and transmission. The automatic transmission illustration shows it as efficiently simple, subtly hiding its actual complication.

In keeping with the times, everything was given a slick 1950s name: Coloramic interiors, Turbo-Fire V-8, Blue Flame 136, Blue Flame 123, Powerglide. The cars were "new when coming, new when passing, new when going."

Other good technical information included clear and true illustrations of Chevrolet's somewhat superior front and rear glass designs and of the longstanding GM Recirculating-Ball steering gear, which replaced the stiffer Saginaw units still found on Chevrolet and Pontiacs in the early 1950s.

Conveniently found at the back of the book is an efficient, easy-to-read, model-by-model form with spaces where the dealer could fill in prices for his Chevrolets and competing prices for equivalent Ford and Plymouth models. The form's introduction stresses local price. A space for Chevrolet's 150 four-door sedan is listed next to spaces for the Ford Mainline and Plymouth Plaza models and their local prices.

For any question the customer could dream up, the salesman could quickly turn to the book's index.

COMPARISONS

The goal of *Fingertip Facts for the 1955 Chevrolet* was to help dealers outsell the competition. While some of the information in the book is truly legitimate and engaging, there are plenty of instances in which Chevrolet decided to sling a little bull.

CHEVROLET VS. FORD

Reasonable:

The Ford's wheelbase was only a half-inch longer than Chevrolet's, but "Chevrolet's overhangs are over three inches less than Ford's, making the cars' handling and parking easier. Similarly, although the Chevrolet is wider inside, the Ford is bulkier with an outside width of 76 inches, 2 inches more than the Chevrolet."

Smaller turning circle: "Chevrolet can make a complete turn in a street only 38 feet wide. The street would have to widened by three feet before Ford could make the same turn."

Broader rear wheel tread.

More head room: "Although Ford's height is greater, the Chevrolet's average head room is one inch more than the Ford's."

More hip room: "Although the Fords had a broader outside, the Chevrolet has a broader inside."

Greater entrance room.

Greater vision area: "Chevrolet provides 166 more square-inches of glass area than Ford."

Larger side windows. Larger rear window.

Better weight distribution.

Less work per horsepower: "No matter what power team is used, Ford engines must pull more weight per horsepower than Chevrolet engines."

Separate rear quarter windows: "Chevrolet provides the modern vision and style advantages of separate rear quarter windows in all four-door sedans. Ford four-door sedans do not have his feature."

Wraparound rear quarter windows in station wagons.

Clearly visible automatic transmission selector quadrant: "Chevrolet's quadrant is clustered with the speedometer high on the instrument panel. Ford's is near the base of the steering column."

Park and neutral starts: "It is not necessary, as in the Ford, to shift the Chevrolet automatic transmission selector from park to neutral before starting the car. Chevrolet starts can be made in either park or neutral."

Automatic choke: Ford still used hand-operated choke.

Central glove compartment: "Chevrolet's glove compartment is within easy reach of both the driver and the front seat passenger. Ford's glove compartment is located at the extreme right of the instrument panel."

Electric windshield wipers: "Ford still offers only a vacuum pump."

Concentric steering column: Ford still had a separate rod for the gearshift that was in full view.

Gasoline filter in fuel tank: "Filter prevents water from getting into fuel line. Ford's filter is at the fuel pump and does not prevent water from entering and freezing in the fuel line."

Chevrolet's 12-volt electrical system was better in all ways.

Chevrolet offered two six-cylinder engines with more power and torque in both than Ford's 1955 six.

Center roof bow. "All Chevrolet steel top is strengthened by a rigid roof bow. In all sedan and station wagon models, this bow connects the center posts. Ford does not have this safety feature."

Dubious:

Lower car height: "Chevrolet's loaded height 60.5 inches, one-half inch less than the Ford for better appearance."

One-inch taller windshield.

Heavier basic car: "Chevrolet's lowest-price conventional six weighs 60 pounds more than a comparable Ford."

Style and appearance: "Ford's body resembles that of the previous year."

Integral headlight hoods: "Chevrolet's handsome headlight hoods are smoothly formed into the graceful front fenders—without any disturbing break in the painted surface. Ford's protruding hoods are formed in the headlight rims with unsightly breaks where the rims clamp on the fenders."

Dip-down beltline: "Chevrolet's distinctive Dip-down beltline is one of the many styling notes that make Chevrolet a truly modern car. Ford's conservative beltline is high and straight."

CHEVROLET VS. PLYMOUTH

Reasonable:

More compact length: Chevrolet and Plymouth both had 115-inch wheelbases, but "Chevrolet's overhang is eight inches less than Plymouth['s], making handling and parking easier."

Smaller turning circle: "Chevrolet can make a complete turn in a street only 38 feet wide. The street would have to widened by two feet before Plymouth could make the same turn."

More entrance room.

More head room.

Styling and appearance: "Wider model choice. Chevrolet offers 14 models (15 with the Nomad) and three complete lines. Plymouth offers only 12 with a choice of only two- and four-door sedans in the Savoy lines."

Rear quarter windows in sedans and wrap-around rear quarter windows in wagons.

Chevrolet featured doubled safety with a parking gear, but Plymouth only had the parking brake dating back to Chrysler Corporation's Fluid Drive days.

Chevrolet's 12-volt electrical system was better, and Plymouth would not see its first 12-volt system until the following year.

Chevrolet had two sixes in 1955, and Plymouth only had one. The Plymouth engine was a solid, venerable workhorse of high general quality, but the Chevrolet overhead-valve six was of a much more modern design—especially when it received pressurized oiling and insert bearings in 1954. The valves in the Chevy six were probably cooled a little better than those of any flathead.

Less weight per horsepower.

Chevrolet's Powerglide had controlled-temperature cooling in conjunction with the radiator—probably an advantage over the Plymouth Powerflite, which was not cooled or temperature controlled.

Dubious:

Taller windshield: "Chevrolet's windshield provides a greater view of overhead traffic lights." The difference was only one inch.

Heavier basic car: "Chevrolet's lowest price conventional six weighs 35 pounds more than the comparable Plymouth."

Dip-down beltline: "Dip-down beltline is only one of the many features that label Chevrolet the style leader in its field. Plymouth's conservative beltline is high and straight."

The books touts the all-new Chevrolet V-8, which certainly had its virtues, but it tries to denigrate the Plymouth V-8 by saying that it's just a revamped Dodge truck engine. However, the Chrysler's hemispherical and polyspherical combustion chamber engines are revered to this day for their quality and technological advances.

Chevrolet tried to claim that having only three piston rings per piston was somehow a good thing: "The Plymouth six requires four piston rings per piston."

There's no case that Chevrolet had better brakes than Plymouth in 1955.

The book claims that Chevrolet has "braking dive control" but doesn't explain how it works. One wonders if there was such a thing.

Battery charge and oil pressure warning lights: "These modern indicators are located on the Chevrolet speedometer quadrant and flash only when the oil pressure is low or the battery is not charging. Plymouth still uses dials." No mechanic would agree that an idiot light is better than a gauge, but Chevrolet missed an opportunity to point out a genuine advantage of its gauges over Plymouth's. In the name of appearances, two of Plymouth's dash gauges were directly in front of the passenger on the right-hand end of the dash and invisible to the driver.

Contradictions:

Chevrolet claimed its cars were better because of greater car weight but then claimed pulling less weight per horsepower was better.

Debatable:

Single-key lock system.

Low and reverse side-by-side: "Chevrolet's automatic transmission selector sequence places low and reverse side-by-side for easier rocking out of sand and snow. On the Ford-O-Matic, low and reverse are separated by neutral and drive."

Solid door handles: Ford and Plymouth had hollow undersides on their door handles. This could be legitimate in terms of general quality.

Four-point engine mounting.

Keyless locking. Chevrolet says it's an advantage to be able to lock the car without the key, but one wonders how many locksmiths received overtime getting people into their Chevrolets on freezing nights.

Unlocked off-ignition switch: Chevrolet ignition switches featured one position in which the driver could remove the key without the switch being locked, allowing the option of the car being started without the key. One wonders how many economy-car buyers were getting their Chevrolets valet parked enough for this to be an advantage.

Crank vent panes? Big maybe.

The book does make a good-sounding case that Chevrolet station wagons were roomier.

The book mentions Chevrolet's deep-hub steering wheel but doesn't claim it to be a safety feature.

Continued from page 41

By 1960, Chevrolet had reversed the trend against the competition with a clean, somewhat more conservative update of the 1959 body. Its styling did well against the dowdy, horizontally finned Ford, which seemed a poor imitation of the 1959 Chevrolet, and the wacky, snarling, shark-finned Plymouth.

The newsmakers of 1960 were the Big Three's all-new compact cars in the economy-car class. Ford released the cute Falcon. Chrysler presented the sturdy, high-tech Valiant, a car that was not yet truly a member of the Plymouth division. But the mold-breaker was Chevrolet's rear-engine, six-cylinder, air-cooled Corvair, which set its sights on Volkswagen's burgeoning market. Billed as both high-tech and economical, the Corvair's engine weight was carried over the rear wheels. Dealers enjoyed demonstrating the car's capabilities to customers by driving through muddy fields and snow, although dealers in cold climates reported that the Corvair's light front end and body pan would climb on top of the snow like a sled. Corvair did well for Chevrolet, selling 250,000 its first year. Updates came quickly as performance versions took on names like Spyder-Monza and pumped output up to 180 horsepower by adding more carburetors and turbochargers.

Full-sized Chevrolets took on a clean, attractive boxiness through the early 1960s, and nicely trimmed Impala hardtops had a natural sleekness out of their pressed-and-creased body shells. The 194-cubic-inch displacement from the 1920s made its return on 1962's Chevy II. The well-styled, unit-bodied compact was conceived as a more direct and conventional competitor with the Falcon and Valiant and included an optional 153-ci, four-cylinder engine that predicted the trends of the 1970s and 1980s. Service departments reported that the Chevy II was a reliable, trouble-free car, but in reality, the car had an iffy body quality and totally inadequate rear suspension. Chevy IIs did well, selling better in some locales than others, but the dealers were far happier with the 1964 appearance of the Chevelle. It was larger than

the Chevy II and smaller than the full-sized Chevrolets but had the same full-frame and general quality of the larger offerings. While Chevy II Novas had been fitted with V-8s, the Chevelles carried V-8 power and weight much more safely. When fitted with a six-cylinder powerplant, the Chevelle was nearly as economical as the Chevy II. The Chevelle bit into Chevy II sales quickly and deeply. Many dealers agree with some automotive journalists who suggested the 1964 Chevelle succeeded because it was the return of the 1955 Chevrolet in terms of size, weight, simplicity, and features—an easy-to-handle economy car that would get up and move on the new superhighways. Dealers

often pointed mothers in the direction of Chevelle station wagons, which provided lots of room for groceries and youngsters that the Chevy II did not, and which were easier to handle and park than a full-size wagon. In 1965, the full-size Chevrolets received one of their most appealing updates in history, sporting fastback styling on hardtops; sleeker, more aerodynamic-looking noses; and more rounded edges. There was no hint of the box that full-size Chevrolets had been for the previous four years. Also new for 1965 was an updated Corvair body, and its styling themes quickly showed up on Chevelles in 1966 as well as on the new muscular Camaro in 1967. While the Camaro is generally thought

Nostalgia for the mid-twentieth-century car culture has grown since the 1980s. Many Chevrolet dealership items have become sought-after collectibles, including these Chevrolet promotional model cars that were used as giveaways and gifts for the press. These models often found their way into the hands of children and have become quite rare. Fortunately, the 1963 Corvette Stingray, 1965 Chevrolet pickup, and 1984 Corvette pictured here have a safe home with a Flint, Michigan, collector. *Jamie Kelly*

Other than the mid-size, six-cylinder Nova, Chevrolet's only weapon against the Japanese invasion was its Vega, a good-looking, four-cylinder car with better body quality and comfort than the Hondas and Toyotas of the time. The Vega's aluminum engine was fragile and troublesome. It was also victim of the car world's earliest electronic problems. One of the culprits was a unit designed to shut the engine off if it lost oil pressure. Its poor quality would cause the plug to fall off, and the engine would stop no matter where it was, leaving the driver with no idea that putting the plug back on was the simple cure. Unfortunately, by the time the American makers produced reliable small cars, the gas crunch had passed, and the public wanted big cars again.

The economy improved in the 1980s, and the American car companies got better at producing a car for every taste and economic need. But the gee-whiz era—with the excitement of announcement days, pride in truly improved models, and ease of service work—was long gone. During the 1990s and into the twenty-first century, cars have improved greatly, but models come and go in a blur, none of them standing out like the Hot Ones. Through it all, most dealers openly stated their hope for the American car companies to begin marketing themselves on their history. A few companies have since run clips from decades-old commercials and revived long-ago model names that conjure images of two-tone paint and heavy, toothy chrome grills. Whether the companies develop this approach or not, dealerships are openly reminding the public of their own histories, and even if the corporations never cooperate, the dealerships will stand as proud family businesses that have weathered many storms. Even if the car business is never as simple or as much fun as it once was, the dealerships, their customers, and nostalgic car collectors can look to the past for the atmosphere their grandfathers knew. Buyers of brand-new cars can listen to the stories and absorb the history that made modern-day cars available and appreciate the past legacy and current efforts of the American Chevrolet dealer.

of as a muscle car, many were sold with six-cylinder engines as sporty economy cars akin to the Ford Mustangs that had been storming the highways.

By the late 1960s, millions of baby boomers had reached car-buying age, As a result, Chevrolet had cars on five platforms in an attempt to reach a public that was becoming harder to read and more fragmented in tastes. Young people wanted flash and dash. Families wanted practical cars that didn't embarrass them. And older people wanted large, elegant cars. Mixed in were the rebels who wanted anti-establishment vehicles in the form of muscle cars or environmentally sound economy cars. The car choices may have been more diverse, but the general quality of all American cars was noticeably slipping. As the cars were loaded down with more accessories and crude emissions devices, they developed new problems that mystified service departments, independent garages, and shade-tree mechanics. The end was in sight for do-it-yourself repairs, and those inclined toward nostalgia started to collect antique cars for their simple virtues.

The turbulence of the 1970s started off with serious economic problems. The federal government took the final steps toward taking U.S. currency completely off the gold standard. It instituted wage and price controls, which prevented dealers from cutting employees' wages (and raised prices to pay them). And it initiated paper and metal drives to make up for shortages. The stage was set for the auto industry's second Great Depression. The changes in the value of U.S. currency and the resulting OPEC oil embargo caused a gas crunch. This was disastrous for Chevrolet dealers who had inventories of full-size Caprice station wagons and pickup trucks, many with big-block V-8s.

When the public wanted large cars, the industry had them, and when the public suddenly wanted small economy cars, the industry had to hurry and catch up to the Japanese, who just happened to be sitting there with the right thing at the right time.

(L–R) Engineering genius Charles Kettering; GM chairman Alfred P. Sloan; GM vice president and noted philanthropist C. S. Mott; Chevrolet division head of sales William Holler; 1940s GM president C. E. Wilson; Chevrolet division president M. E. Coyle. Circa 1940. *Holler family collection*

52

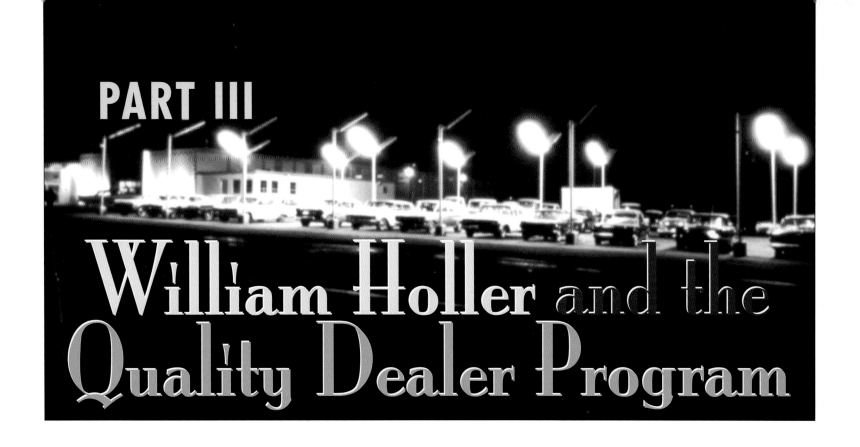

PART III

William Holler and the Quality Dealer Program

By 1949, the beautiful, newly bodied Chevrolets arrived on car lots. In spite of Studebaker's all-new, smooth-sided designs with wraparound glass and Hudson's innovative step-down architecture, General Motors still set the most popular styling trends at that time. Even low-priced Chevrolets shared the corporation's jet-age styling with blended, balanced, curvaceous lines and tasteful trim accenting advanced shapes that pleased the eye. The styling made the models from the year before seem like prewar dinosaurs and reflected America's postwar confidence in a bright technological future.

Under the skin was a different story. Chevrolet's 1949 drivetrain dated to 1928. It had babbitt-rod engine bearings and nonpressurized splash oiling. The enclosed driveshafts made universal joints and clutches time-consuming to work on. And its extremely low rear-axle ratios made speeds over 45 to 50 miles per hour rough on the engine. In many ways, the new automobiles were still prewar cars.

The 1949 Plymouth had a pressurized oil system from the late 1920s and engine bearings dating back to the early 1930s, along with open driveshafts, better rear-axle ratios, and the best brakes of any low-priced car. The Nash 600 was surely underpowered, but it would give low-demand, daily drivers an honest 25 to 30 miles per gallon. Ford's chassis had finally gotten out of the 1920s, and while its engines were outdated and known for overheating, V-8-powered Fords, available with Borg-Warner overdrive, were certainly better road cars than Chevrolets on the four-lane highways that were quickly crisscrossing the continent.

Much to the surprise of gearheads, Chevrolet outsold everyone in 1949. Classic car collectors who look at automotive substance first couldn't understand the popularity of the Chevrolets. But the seeds of the cars' postwar success over more technologically advanced cars were planted in the 1930s when Chevrolet cemented customer loyalty by addressing the human

> "Finally, William Holler came on, changed the fervor of the meeting entirely, and gave the dealers a lift. My father, driving back from the meeting, was wondering how he was going to meet payroll for the following week. He had employees sleeping in the building. It was quite a depressing time, but Holler seemed to have the ability to inspire some to go on."
>
> — *Chap Morris Sr., William L. Morris Chevrolet, Fillmore, California*

"At that time, my father would come back from any sales meeting William Holler would have, and someone was going to buy a car. Bill Holler had a knack for getting people enthused to sell. It was the Quality Dealer Program, and it's too bad we got away from it. Take care of the customer, what a concept! It was one of the best things to ever happen to Chevrolet, and they should bring it back lock, stock, and barrel—just as it was."

—Jerry Holz, Holz Motors, Hales Corners, Wisconsin

William E. Holler. *Holler family collection*

being. Chevrolet was known for addressing each customer's thoughts, feelings, and concerns, and consumers lined up out of loyalty to Chevrolet dealers in spite of the cars' weaknesses. Chevrolet's customer loyalty was obvious well into the 1960s and is possibly still an underlying influence in the twenty-first century. The continuing loyalty is due in large part to William Holler, the head of Chevrolet sales in the 1930s, and his Quality Dealer Program.

ROUGH BEGINNINGS
William Holler was born in Buffalo, New York, just before the dawn of the twentieth century and grew up in New York City. Family lore has it that Holler was the leader of a small street gang in his teens, during a time when the Italian Black Hand and Irish Five Points gangs were organizing themselves into tough, deadly criminal enterprises. Holler avoided a life of crime and took his street-level toughness to the healthier outlet of the boxing ring.

"He used to be a boxer at the YMCA, and if he got a bloody nose, he would suck it in and spit it into the other guy's face," says Roger Holler Jr. of his grandfather. "He wasn't a guy you wanted to mess with. He was in his car one day in about 1928 or 1929, and he was driving down a muddy road where you had to drive with your wheels in the ruts and the bottom of the car scraping on the hump in the middle. There was a truck coming, and my grandfather wouldn't move over, and the truck wouldn't move over. So he pulled both the truck drivers out of the cab and beat the you-know-what out of them."

William Holler was married in the 1920s, and his young wife, Cora, helped him improve his ability to read, write, and do basic math as the couple struggled to get by.

"My grandparents lived above a little food stand and deli," Roger Holler tells. "My grandfather made a little fish hook on a string to bring up apples and stuff from the deli because they

54

couldn't afford food. They had a cage to catch pigeons with, and that was their Sunday lunch."

DISCOVERED

Although Roger Holler does not recall hearing his grandfather's deepest thoughts on the subject, it seems that by the time William Holler

Decades after his passing, William Holler's passionate style and powerful advice still speak through his 1952 book *Step Out and Sell!* Holler contended that history held the greatest lessons in strength and perseverance and offered examples ranging from the tales of Hannibal to stories of Napoleon. Once a tough street kid and fearless YMCA boxer, Holler developed a sentiment for the arts and sciences. His book points to Michelangelo, poet John Milton, and Sir Isaac Newton as men who endured long-term hardships to accomplish their later acclaimed works.

reached 30 years of age, he had dedicated himself to saving young men from some of the rougher times of his own youth and became an effective booster for the YMCA.

Holler's speeches were riveting. Witnesses report an hour passing like minutes when Holler spoke, and when he was finished, the audience was on his side and burning to boost the YMCA. In 1929, Holler finished one such speech in Buffalo, New York, oblivious to the impression he had just made. C. S. Mott, the head of General Motors, was in the audience, and he hired the former New York City street kid, a man who had just learned to read, to be a general sales manager at Chevrolet.

THE QUALITY DEALER PROGRAM

The good news of Holler's new job at Chevrolet was tempered by the bad news that the stock market had crashed and plunged America into the Great Depression.

Holler instituted the Quality Dealer Program, which required Chevrolet dealers to be upstanding citizens in their communities. A Chevrolet franchise would not be granted to anyone with a criminal record, and longtime dealers report that they had to periodically fill out forms reporting their civic activities to Chevrolet. The program strongly urged dealers to be members of churches and school boards and to be active supporters of youth activities. The dealers had to give quality service to all their customers, starting with the neat, clean appearance of their dealerships. The Quality

"Bill Holler put Chevrolet on the map. He got all the dealers to be on his side by working on their side and by taking and following through with all of the suggestions from the dealers. He would have dealer meetings right out on the sales floor for all the dealers in our area, and he could really fire up you up, I tell you that, right out. The Quality Dealer Program was one of his great ideas. It appealed to the salesmen because quality was important then. Mr. Holler was gifted in his phrasing, and he inspired the salesmen and dealers to do a better job."

— Hal Smith, Smith Chevrolet, Atlanta, Georgia

Dealer Program encouraged dealers to find creative ways to serve customers outside the showroom. One dealer who excelled at this was William L. Morris, a man who worked in California's farm belt. He cemented customer loyalty by going out every morning with a big battery and jump starting all the farmers' tractors for the day.

In return for such extra efforts, Holler improved the Chevrolet cars and fought for the dealers.

"He did stuff that the fourteenth floor wouldn't approve because it wasn't in their budget," Roger Holler Jr. relates. "He used to put chrome on the cars and show them to the dealers without approval from GM. When the dealers saw the cars, they expected the chrome to be there. He put the vacuum windshield wipers on the cars and got rid of those little hand-operated

"Building men is management's first responsibility."

—William Holler

The 1950s: Laws, Dealers, and the Continuing Debate

Car dealerships in the 1950s are remembered for sweeping neon decor, expansive glass showrooms, colorful jet-age style resting on whitewall tires, and exciting model unveilings, but even the thrill of announcement day couldn't eliminate the dealers' worries.

The immediate postwar years may have given car dealers some of their most successful and fondly remembered days. But the period also handed them turmoil the public didn't always see. They faced difficulties in getting sufficient amounts of product to satisfy customers and provide choice. Cars were often shipped with accessories the dealer didn't order, making them harder to sell to the public. Bribery and waiting list shenanigans on the parts of both dealers and the public threatened to damage the business climate for the honest dealers. On top of it all, dealers were pressured to build larger dealership facilities and purchase expensive new signs without the promise of either one generating more business.

The federal government stepped in and passed two of the most important laws in the history of car dealerships. The dealers universally cheered one of the laws, and the other is still debated nearly a half-century later.

Dealers Get Their "Day in Court."
The U.S. Code calls Title 15, Chapter 27, *Automobile Dealer Suits Against Manufacturers*, but the dealers called it the "Day in Court Law."

With the increased business for the American auto industry came increased demands on dealers to keep up with the times. Dealers felt that manufacturers canceled dealer franchises without much mercy. Longstanding dealers seem to agree that smaller, rural dealerships were canceled most commonly, ostensibly for not maintaining sufficient sales volume or not participating in the manufacturers' programs, some of which cost money.

In 1955, Wyoming Senator Joseph C. O'Mahoney held hearings in which dealers, including a number from General Motors, aired their complaints. The resulting law granted dealers the right to sue if the manufacturers canceled their franchises without showing cause, which the law viewed as acting against the interests of "good faith."

GM's Operations Policy Committee acted quickly and decided in one hurried Sunday meeting to extend the contracts of all GM franchise dealers from one to five years. *Time* mentioned this decision in its article naming General Motors president Harlow Curtice "Man of the Year" for 1955. Among his many other traits, *Time* felt that Curtice acted decisively in response to the policy committee's recommendations in spite of his personal feelings that the dealers' complaints were overstated.

The Window Sticker Law
Manufacturers' Suggested Retail Price has become such a familiar concept that it's known simply as the MSRP. The MSRP made its first appearance in the automotive world in 1958, glued to the window of each new car. It gave the car's base price, shipping charges, and an itemized list of all optional equipment. For its first few years, people called it the Monroney sticker, named for Senator Mike Monroney of Oklahoma who chaired the Senate Subcommittee on Automobile Marketing Practices. Monroney's bill became U.S. Code Title 15, Chapter 28, *Disclosure of Automobile Information*.

With the end of World War II and its resulting shortages, throngs of car-hungry consumers waited patiently for new cars. They were often shocked when they found that the cars cost more than previously quoted. The cars were sometimes loaded down with accessories the buyer didn't want and, in many cases, the dealer didn't want either. If the dealer wanted to have cars to sell and keep his allotment, he had to take the accessories that came with the cars and pass the costs along to the customers. Other scenarios, of course, included unscrupulous dealers advertising a car for sale only to raise the price on customers once they were in the showroom, suddenly revealing dubious shipping charges and other ambiguous fees. The Monroney sticker made these practices next to impossible, forcing dealers to reveal all the costs to the customer.

Many dealers applauded the law because they felt their industry needed some cleaning up at both the manufacturer and dealership levels, and that honest dealers needed to be protected from the detrimental effects that dishonest dealers wrought on the profession.

Individually and through various car dealer associations, other dealers argued passionately against the law as written, citing issues the law did not address. Wyoming Chevrolet dealer Bud Webster explains that, while the Monroney sticker controlled what the dealer could charge the public for a car, the law did not address what the manufacturer could charge the dealer. The factory could raise its wholesale price to the dealer, but the dealer could not raise his price to the public. Dealers typically had a 24 percent markup on a car and left a lot of room for bargaining on final price and trade-in value, but factories raised their prices, squeezed the dealer profit margins, and eliminated much of the dealers' bargaining room. In some ways, the Monroney law took away an honest dealer's ability to give a customer a good deal when necessary to make a sale. If, for example, an insistent customer maintained that his trade-in was of a certain value in spite of the dealer knowing it was worth considerably less, the headroom of the pre-Monroney-law world allowed the dealer to raise the retail price of the new car to absorb some of the profit he was giving up to the buyer by taking in an overvalued trade-in.

Some dealers, such as Dick Stowers of Culberson-Stowers Chevrolet in Pampa, Texas, and Jerry Holz of Holz Motors in Hales Corners, Wisconsin, take a more philosophical view of the business. The way they see it, a dealer must be prepared to work with whatever the factory, the government, and the world throw at them.

This beautiful brass and amber ashtray has decorated the office of Felix Chevrolet in Los Angeles since the early 1930s. "To my good friend Bill Felix, from his friend William E. Holler" is inscribed on the ashtray.

wipers. He did things GM didn't approve, but once they were on the cars, they had to be on there from then on. He wanted to have things on the cars that Ford didn't have. He was in the position to make changes to the cars, and the dealers would see it, like it, and GM would have to produce the cars that way. He was a real innovator."

Holler made the dealers feel as though he was on their side by forming the Dealer Council. The group was made up of prominent dealers whose job it was to listen to other dealers and take their suggestions to Chevrolet and General Motors.

"My grandfather didn't care if a dealership had a car storage problem. If your store was clean and you were selling, he wanted you to stay where you were, and that saved a lot of dealers during the hard times in the '30s and '40s. As long as it was presentable and clean, he wanted the dealers to stay where they were and have enough capital to survive hard times because everything cycles over a period of time. It wasn't like today where all the companies want the dealers to build new facilities all the time. He fought for the dealers—to protect the dealers' allotments of cars and other things the dealers needed from the factory. He put his job on the line many times."

Holler was famous throughout the Chevrolet organization for his powerful slogan "Go out

"Whenever Bill Holler drove around Detroit, and he saw a Chevrolet that had body damage, he would get the license number and refer it to a local dealer for repairs. His talks were about an hour long and it only felt like ten minutes. When I started in 1937, I was only 25 years old. I had stars in my eyes, and I really went for that stuff."

— *Bud Webster, Webster Chevrolet, Cody, Wyoming*

and build an empire for your sons and your sons' sons." He established the Dealers' Sons School where new dealers could formally learn the fundamentals of dealership operations, customer service, and basic business skills. The establishment still exists under the name General Motors School of Marketing and Management.

"Because he was self-educated with my grandmother's help, he started the Dealers' Sons School so other people wouldn't have to start in the business without an education like he'd had to do—to give the dealer the education to read the financial statements. He wanted people to struggle and work for what they got, but he wanted to give people the tools to work with and not have to find the tools themselves."

THE IDEAS

William Holler would be described today as a workaholic. He did nearly 100 speaking engagements a year. His dynamic speeches held audiences in rapt silence that erupted into thundering applause when he finished.

"There was one meeting he held in a room the size of a basketball arena," Roger Holler tells, "and when he was finished speaking, the people were standing on the tables—not on the chairs, on the *tables!*"

In today's infomercial-packed, seminar-crazed, self-help media culture, William Holler's advice might sound familiar and tired. But when up against the Great Depression's genuine perils, Chevrolet dealers needed fierce encouragement of a kind they hadn't heard before. They needed a man who believed in what he was saying, believed in the dealers, and had proven himself to be on their side against the competition and, sometimes, GM's internal decision makers. Faced with real threat and blessed with an honest leader, Chevrolet's dealers listened carefully to what Holler had to say.

While no recordings or transcripts have been obtained, a glimpse of Holler's speaking style can be gleaned from his book *Step Out and Sell!* which he wrote in 1952, six years

"Go out and build an empire for your sons and your sons' sons."

—*William Holler*

after his retirement. It carries much of the phrasing Chevrolet dealers found so innovative in the prewar world. Holler wrote:

What is your philosophy of life and living? Are you a *doer* or a *doubter*? Do you *work* for things, or do you just *wait* for them? Are you a *force* or an *obstruction*?... Know people, and like them. I believe it is a waste of time for a man who does not like

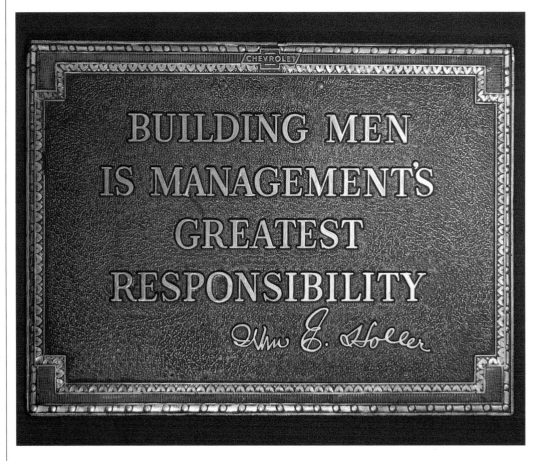

One of Holler's most famous sayings still hangs on the wall of William L. Morris Chevrolet in Fillmore, California.

58

SUCCESS
IS
GOOD MANAGEMENT
IN ACTION

REMEMBERED

Longtime Chevrolet dealer Bud Webster of Cody, Wyoming, bought a failing Chevrolet franchise in 1937 when he was only 25 years old and considers himself fortunate to have heard William Holler speak in person. Webster also witnessed what could have been one of the very few times that William Holler lost the attention of an audience.

"We had a zone meeting after Great Falls and Salt Lake City zones merged, and Bill Holler was the speaker," Bud Webster remembers.

CHEVROLET

NEVER
FORGET
A CUSTOMER
—
NEVER
LET HIM
FORGET
YOU

people to try to be a salesman. If you like people, you are tolerant of what they think and what they do. You are interested in people. You want to be of some help to them. You want to serve them. . . . People pay huge returns to those who serve them well. . . . Pick your own field—think of music, of art, of athletics, or authorship. In all of them, you'll find the same philosophy of giving every last ounce of energy and effort to the task—of *giving* rather than *getting*. You'll find Caruso practicing hour after hour every day for 30 years to develop voice tones just a little richer. You'll remember that Michelangelo endured agony hour after hour, day after day, for four-and-a-half years as he lay flat on his back to paint the supremely beautiful ceiling of the Sistine Chapel. You'll think of Milton, who was blind, stringing parallel wires to guide his pen as he wrote the immortal *Paradise Lost*. . . . It takes the ability to say, 'How can I do this better?' instead of 'How can I get more for myself?'. . . . It is those people who give the most that come out ahead when the last score is tallied.

Holler came to love reading biographies, and he relayed much of what he learned. He wrote short, gripping, detailed accounts of Hannibal's armies enduring countless obstacles and agonies as they crossed the Alps to attack the Roman Empire, which had grown too comfortable. And he shared tales of Napoleon breaking the eighteenth century's rules of war by aiming cannons into the mass of enemy soldiers and horses, having believed it was more civilized to end a battle quickly than to have it drag out.

Holler's wisdom has found its way from unknown Chevrolet dealerships into the Tom Meleo collection.

OK Used Cars

*An effective tool that was, in some ways,
more beautiful than Chevrolet's new-car merchandising.*

"Louis Chevrolet says this car is OK!" proclaims a Chevrolet ad from the 1920s. Some say this may have been the inspiration for Chevrolet's OK Used Cars program. Photographs of Chevrolet dealerships from the 1930s often show used-car lots adorned with giant signs shouting "OK'd Used Cars," making "OK" into a past-tense verb.

"New car and truck sales are directly dependent on the ability of a dealer to move used cars and trucks," says the *OK Used Car and Truck Merchandising Materials for Chevrolet Dealers* catalog from 1960. "There is no one factor more vital to continued success than a dealer's skill in merchandising the volume of trade-ins that may be required in his local market."

Ford competed with a used-car program called "A-1," but no other car company's used-car program had imagery as striking as Chevrolet's OK Used Cars. In some cases, OK Used Cars signs, decor, and sales paraphernalia eclipsed Chevrolet's new-car promotional materials in terms of artistic beauty and colorful presentation. Being an economy brand for most of its history, Chevrolet's signs were modest statements. The simple, steely-blue bowtie with C-H-E-V-R-O-L-E-T spelled out in white letters on a blue background was humble even when trimmed in neon. On the other hand, OK Used Cars signs dazzled. If a dealer installed the whole OK Used Cars treatment, his used-car lot could make his new-car lot invisible if he wasn't careful. OK Used Cars lots splashed on the program's official colors—red, yellow, and blue—and the used-car lots were

From the Tom Meleo collection.

often rimmed with smaller, drum-shaped OK signs of flashing neon with glowing, back-lit, silhouetted panels. In the 1940s, Chevrolet offered a special prefabricated OK Used Cars closing office that was trimmed in all the official colors and could be erected in a day using only a small corner of the used-car lot. Available in three sizes, the dealer could close the used-car deal in the same comfort as the new-car deal.

Pat Matlach was an independent used-car dealer for several decades in Victorville, California. Matlach submits that most new-car dealers kept their new cars indoors to protect them from the weather. OK Used Cars' bright decor was meant to bring the vibrant color of the showroom to used-car inventories usually stored outdoors. Matlach adds that prior to the

early 1960s, many small dealerships had only three or four demonstrators on their showroom floors, while outdoors sat a fleet of trade-ins that needed to move quickly. In some cases, it was also dealership policy for the salesman not to get his commission on a new-car sale until the trade-in on that deal sold.

Behind all the glitz was a fairly simple warranty program. While the details changed many times throughout the decades, the basics were that an "OK" used car had been inspected in accordance with a checklist called the "OK Used Vehicle Inspection and Reconditioning Guide" and that all its major components were expected to last for a reasonable amount of time.

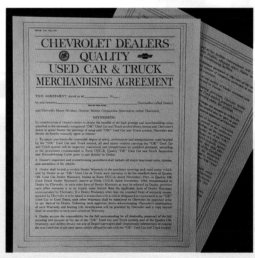

Bob McDorman of McDorman Chevrolet in Canal Winchester, Ohio, signed a contract like this one when he first took on the OK Used Cars program along with his Bowtie franchise in 1965. *Bob McDorman collection*

 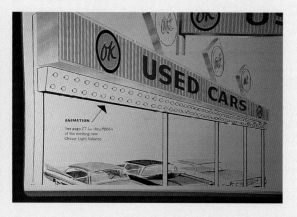

From plain painted background screens to the dazzling full-treatment of the "Spectacular," the OK Used Cars catalog offered the Chevrolet dealer a wide variety of strong imagery to catch the passing eye. *Bob McDorman collection*

Bob McDorman's collection showcases many of the sign designs used in the OK Used Cars program. The merchandising included valances streaked with many yards of neon, some as wide as the car lot. *Bob McDorman collection*

If a car didn't pass all the requirements of the OK Used Car inspection, it would be billed as a "Good Value" used car to be sold explicitly "as is."

A sample OK Used Car dealer instruction package from 1973 states:

The terms and conditions of the policy are spelled out clearly on the OK Used Vehicle Dealer Warranty document. Basically, they provide two types of benefits: 1) 100 percent coverage for 30 days or 2,000 miles, under normal use from the dealership of purchase; and 2) 24 months at a 15 percent parts and labor discount from the dealership of purchase. (In addition, other participating dealers generally offer special savings on parts and labor.) The program provides a new, high level of warranty coverage for prospective owners and should be explained to every used-car prospect. The OK Used Car Vehicle Warranty is the last word on used-car dependability. It should be your last word in an effective sales presentation.

This was an improvement over the OK Used Car offerings of 1960 when used cars were covered for 30 days but only 1,000 miles, and the warranty only offered to pay 50 percent of the costs of parts and labor.

The program covered tires in a very limited way and gave the customer a 25 percent discount on tires replaced under the program only if the customer was paying cash for the balance.

While the 1973 version boasted a 24-month warranty, the guarantee was a bit iffy because, while the car was covered very well for the first 30 days, the remaining 23 months only offered a 15 percent discount on parts and labor. This 15 percent discount was sometimes irrelevant because dealership labor rates at the dealerships were substantially higher than at independent garages.

The program faded away in the early 1980s, but two decades later, it's not unusual to see Chevrolet dealerships still sporting the colorful signs. Many can be found cheerfully touting OK Used Cars as attention-grabbing monuments to a time when dealership décor was a little more fun. In some cases, the signs may honor the grandfather who put them up originally.

Tom Meleo of California, Pinky Randall of Michigan, and Chevrolet dealer Bob McDorman of Ohio are all prominent Chevrolet memorabilia collectors. While their collections encompass Chevrolet materials of all kinds,

they all seem especially attracted to the bright, colorful artifacts of OK Used Cars. The Chevrolet enthusiast and collector can look back at the vivid objects of OK Used Cars and imagine a time when buying a used car at a Chevrolet dealership was as colorful as any new-car announcement day.

A 1966 OK Used Cars magazine ad showing a 1964 Chevrolet deemed "OK" and presented to happy used-car shoppers. *Bob McDorman collection*

Although it was technologically troublesome early in the model run, the 1932 model may be one of the first Chevrolets to be legitimately called beautiful. Reportedly, William Holler insisted that Chevrolet improve the look of its product by adding chrome accents and improvements like vacuum windshield wipers. He showed the spruced-up cars to the dealers before allowing the decision makers at GM to see them. Once the dealers had seen the improvements, they expected them to be there and weren't interested in accepting cars without them. From the Tom Meleo collection.

"Holler was a dynamic. He inspired you. He would ball up his hands and push his fist up in the air to emphasize his point. We ran out of the meetings—didn't walk—we ran out of the meetings to call our dealerships to inspire them, too. 'Beat the Ford!' was Holler's motto."

—*Larry Dimmitt Jr., Dimmitt Chevrolet, Clearwater, Florida*

"It was at the Hotel Utah in Salt Lake City, which was a beautiful hotel and now is the headquarters of the Mormon church. The meeting was on the roof, and it was a beautiful day and a wonderful atmosphere. There was a wing of the Hotel Utah opposite the roof area where we were having this open-air meeting, not more than about 50 feet away. There was a woman in there changing her clothes, and here we had about 100 people listening to Bill Holler making his talk, but he lost the attention of most of the audience because at least a third of the guys were looking over there, watching this woman taking her clothes off."

Webster, who still has a Quality Dealer Program plaque on his office wall that reads, "Building men is management's first responsibility," thinks of William Holler often and made a decision several years after Holler's retirement based on something he had heard Holler say.

"He would give a talk, and it would last an hour, but you'd swear it wasn't more than ten minutes," Webster recalls. "He was a stem-winder—an innovator. There's never been anything else like him that I've ever heard. I thought he was a great guy. I heard Holler say, 'I'm going to make Chevrolet the best franchise in the world, and that includes Coca-Cola,

Southern Arizona Auto Company

Above: The Southern Arizona Auto Company got its start in 1908 in the now-deserted town of Courtland.

Right: The Southern Arizona Auto Company had gone Chevrolet by the 1930s. This photo, seen here for the first time since the late 1930s, was reproduced from its original wooden-block, halftone process and provides a glimpse into a long-ago showroom.

which has always been known as the best franchise of any.' As a result of his saying that, [I thought of the Coca-Cola franchise in this area] which covered about 25 percent of the state of Wyoming, and I went over to sell the manager of the Coca-Cola franchise a car. I didn't sell him a car, but we went to a bar and had a few drinks, and he said, 'You know, Bud, I'm 60 years old, and I want to get out of the business.' He had all these trucks, buildings, and real estate in Thermopolis, Wyoming. I asked him what he wanted for it, and he said $100,000. We met at his lawyer's office, and we entered into a sales agreement. I called my wife and asked her to go to the bank and bring $10,000

over to Thermopolis. I gave him the $10,000 down and bought the Coca-Cola business, which I kept for 36 years. In 1960, we moved the Coca-Cola business from Thermopolis to Cody. It turned out to be a good investment, and I sold it in 1979. I seriously doubt that I would have ever bought Coca-Cola if I hadn't heard William Holler call it the best franchise on the market."

William Holler retired to Mount Dora, Florida, in 1946 and continued his efforts to help youth by setting up activities and essay contests for scholarships. Roger Holler's eyes tear up when he thinks of his grandfather, who passed away in 1981.

"I've tried to guide my whole life after him," Roger says. "He was gutsy. He was honest, and he was tenacious when he thought he was right. I try to take all the qualities that he had and pass them on to my own kids. He was just so remarkable. You always treat your fellow man right. You just know if you're doing the right thing or not. We had all these factory people from Detroit come down for his funeral. There was a little church in Mount Dora, and they had to seat people in the church next door and put a TV in there for it. His funeral packed two churches side by side. One of the guys from the factory said, 'It's like when a tree in falls in the forest. There's an empty void when a big tree falls.' "

The smiling cat of Felix Chevrolet is as familiar to Los Angelinos as the Coliseum or the city hall. The oversized feline took his place at Figueroa and Jefferson in 1958.

PART IV

The Front Lines

Do we want to know what it was, or do we want to know *what it was like?* Both mean a great deal to the devotees of antique cars. Automotive history is hotly argued for accuracy by those who want to know details like who, exactly when, and how. Others, though, want to walk into an aged building, drive an old car, or hear half-remembered tales, and they aren't concerned if some of the names have been forgotten and the dates are only accurate within a decade.

Chevrolet dealers were on the front lines of the automobile battles, and their memories of the cars and trucks they sold and serviced and the customers who bought them cannot be found in the Joe Friday version of history. The dealers were there when the factories handed them gems and lemons, and they were there when times were good and bad. Chevrolet dealers rode the wave of postwar prosperity when, only a decade before, they were taking horses and shotguns as trade-ins. Chevrolet dealers were thrown through the windshields on test drives by customers who hadn't driven automatic transmissions before. And they had driverless cars run amuck in the service departments. They let the Hot Ones speak for themselves but had a lot of explaining to do when Corvair fan belts kept breaking. They knew the cars, the public, and their communities like no one else, and they can explain changing times better than professors with Ph.D.s in history could. The Chevrolet dealer has a business mind and is an accountant, sociologist, psychologist, historian, and mechanic. A Chevrolet dealer is a businessman or -woman with grease under his or her nails and a confident salesperson with the nerves of a tightrope walker.

What follows are the stories of eight dealerships. They're from parts of the U.S. so different from one another that they might as well have been in different countries, but each one is an American Chevrolet dealer.

WILLIAM L. MORRIS CHEVROLET— FILLMORE, CALIFORNIA
Rising from the Ruins of Double Disasters
As if being the new guy in town wasn't bad enough, opening for business on Black Thursday was a cruel twist, contorted further by the seemingly haunted 1929 Chevrolet "International," the car Bill Morris sold on his first day in business. Fifty-eight years later, in the fall of 1987, Morris' descendants bought him a gift, a beautifully preserved 1929 Chevrolet to remind him of his first sale. Ironically, on that day, the stock market crashed again. As far as Morris is concerned, these demure jazz-age economy cars are cosmically connected to world economics.

"We've kept the car ever since," says John Chapman "Chap" Morris Jr., "and the stock market's broken records for being the highest it's ever been. Our intentions are that we're never going to sell that car. I don't think the world wants us to sell that car!"

William L. Morris was born in 1900. His family owned ranches in La Habra, California, and through a chain of events that included divorce and a new stepfather, a 10-year-old Bill Morris found himself on his own. He made his way north to the San Fernando Valley where his family had another ranch. He got a job in a livery stable, and this job shaped the rest of his life.

Fillmore, California, was sleeping peacefully on the night of March 12, 1928, in the midst of the lengthy Santa Clara River Valley. Wealthy farmers and migrant workers, engineers and laborers, and oil and electricity men were all looking forward to spring when the scents of orange blossoms, newly cut alfalfa, and millions of wild flowers would rise from the valley's fertile soil. The rich, the poor, the educated, and the humble didn't know a clock had stopped in an electric company station 20 miles away. A monster had blasted from the Earth at 11:57 P.M. With pitiless, reptilian indifference, it vented its fury on pockets of small-town America. Castaic Junction, Piru, Fillmore, Santa Paula, and Saticoy were ground to bits under the monster's feet. None escaped before the monster slipped quietly into the Pacific Ocean and became invisible.

The St. Francis Dam had exploded. The Los Angeles Aqueduct had been swimming in controversy before and after its completion in 1913 for having "stolen" water from farmers in the Owens Valley, an area a couple hundred miles away, to feed Los Angeles' growing thirst. The Los Angeles Department of Water and Power finished the St. Francis Dam in 1926 as a safety reservoir to continue the flow of water to the city in the event of one of California's common earthquakes. The dam was built on unstable ground from inadequate materials. When it failed, it sent floodwaters moving at speeds of 25 miles per hour. Water found the Santa Clara River bed and roared west. Five hours, 50 miles, and 495 lives later, the deluge had shrunk to 15 feet deep and fell harmlessly into the ocean near Ventura.

A 200-foot-tall section of the concrete dam's face stood alone in the middle of San Francisquito Canyon in 1929. People called it the Tombstone. A few look at it as the omen signaling Black Thursday, or October 29, 1929, when the American stock market crashed and plunged the world into the Great Depression.

A young man opened a Chevrolet dealership in a small town and sold a car on his first day. The man was William L. Morris, and the town was Fillmore, California. Fillmore survived the St. Francis Dam disaster, and William L. Morris Chevrolet survived opening for business on the first day of the Great Depression.

"He was sleeping above the offices of the livery stable, which was also a soda fountain and a gas station," Chap Jr. tells. "The livery stable became a dealership. They started with Fords, and at 14 years old, in 1914, my grandfather sold his first car. He had been working there four years and, by chance, he happened to be there when a customer walked onto the lot and asked him, 'You know all the cars on this lot better than the salesmen, and you're going to tell me the truth. Which one do you think is the best one?' My grandfather said, 'This one over here is the best one. I got to drive it, and it's really nice.' The customer walked in and told the salesman, 'I want to buy *this car*, and I want to buy it from *this kid*.' That's how my grandfather got started."

As a teenager, Bill Morris dreamed of seeing his name high on the wall of his own dealership and receiving the respect of a successful car dealer. By all accounts, this dream was the incentive that made Morris develop the qualities needed to take him to his dream.

Morris worked for the Ford dealer until 1927 when he had a chance to buy half of the interest in the dealership from his employer, Charles B. Chapman, for whom Morris' son and grandson, John Chapman Morris Sr. and Jr., are named. The San Fernando dealership became a Chevrolet franchise, and soon Morris was able to buy out Chapman.

"Chevrolet offered him the franchises up in this area, past the mountains north and west of Los Angeles, which included Fillmore, Santa Paula, Moorpark; and they had a used-car facility up in Newbury Park," Chap Jr. tells. "So he decided to do it, and he opened his doors on October 29, 1929, the day the stock market crashed!"

Morris' wife, Verna, was not at all convinced she wanted to live in the remote farming/railroad town of Fillmore. The ambiance of an eatery called T-Bone Harry's only fueled her negative impression of Fillmore. T-Bone Harry's was an establishment from the cigarette-over-the-grill, hanging-fly-paper, egg-shells-stacked-on-the-counter school of restaurant décor. It was amid the restaurant's defused light and greasy stench that Verna and Bill struck an agreement. If she was not happy in Fillmore by the end of two years, they would leave and start again somewhere else.

William L. Morris Chevrolet's original location at the corner of Central and Santa Clara in Fillmore, California, opened for business on the first day of the Great Depression. Somehow it survived and coexisted peacefully with a Flying-A service station. *William L. Morris Chevrolet collection*

William L. Morris Chevrolet opened at the corner of Central and Santa Clara and coexisted with a Flying A service station. Morris quickly got down to the business of fighting the Great Depression. Chap Jr. explains:

A lot of it was based on integrity. He would get up early in the morning, go out to all the ranches, and jump start all the farmers' tractors. He had what I guess they called a hot-shot battery. So, he built up a relationship with the farming community. He never asked for a dime, and he never took a dime for any of those services. He had been using the same mode of operation down in San Fernando, but he knew he was the new guy in Fillmore, and everybody told him he was going to fail, but his intentions were, and his intestinal fortitude was, that he was not going to quit.

While building customer loyalty, Morris also made the nuts and bolts of the car trade work. Chap Morris Sr. picks up the story:

In 1932, we were really in the heart of the Depression, and he could remember one dealer meeting specifically that they had at the Coconut Grove in Los Angeles and driving there from Fillmore in a '32 Chevrolet, which was quite a feat in itself. He said the meeting was quite depressing because probably half the dealers were there only because Chevrolet hadn't found anyone to buy out their dealerships. When the executives from GM would come onto the stage, you would hear catcalls from the audience—very disrespectful. Finally, William Holler came on, changed the fervor of the meeting entirely, and gave them a lift. His theme was, 'Go and build an empire for your sons and your sons' sons.' My father, driving back from the meeting, was wondering how he was going to meet payroll for the following week. He had employees sleeping in the building. It was quite a depressing time, but Holler seemed to have the ability to inspire some to go on.

The always dapper William L. Morris sold his first new Ford at age 14. *William L. Morris Chevrolet collection*

The citrus industry was the cornerstone of California's Santa Clara River Valley. Bill Morris earned the trust of the community by helping the citrus growers start their tractors on cold mornings. When a farmer needed his next new truck, he went to the nice man who had helped him. *William L. Morris Chevrolet collection*

Holler brought in the Quality Dealer Program, and my father kept a plaque on his wall for many, many years that said, 'Building men is management's greatest responsibility.' You had to meet requirements to be a Chevrolet dealer under that program. If you were a felon, you couldn't get a Chevrolet franchise. They would send out questionnaires annually asking what civic organizations you were a member of toward becoming a solid citizen of your community.

During the Depression, Morris bartered with customers, accepting everything from horses and cows to shotguns. Chap Jr. comments

that small businesses had the freedom to be creative and succeed against the odds, which Bill Morris did.

"We used to have our cars shipped in by train," Chap Sr. explains. "You couldn't get the cars until you paid for them. My father got along really well with the stationmaster, and he would open up the boxcar door so my father could look in there and say to a customer, 'See that car up there. That one could be yours.' And he would sell them while they were still in the boxcars. He'd write the contract on that car, and

then he'd drive to GMAC, and GMAC would give him the cash for the contract. I've heard that he made two, possibly three, trips in a day driving from Fillmore to Wilshire Boulevard in Los Angeles to get the cash for those contracts, with the roads and cars the way they were then, all to get those cars unloaded. I guess he'd drive pretty fast. My father was on his way back from Los Angeles in the middle of the Depression, and he was wondering how he was going to make payroll for that week, which was $75. He really thought he was finished. Down in San

Fernando, he went by a real estate office where he knew the salesman. There was a big ranch in San Fernando that was up for sale at a complete sacrifice. He took his last $25 and got an option to buy the ranch, and he went out Sunday and sold the option for $150 and got enough money to cover his payroll. He was back in business when he opened the doors on Monday."

The Great Depression had been easing, but a crop-killing frost and severe, widespread flooding destroyed millions of dollars in farm revenue throughout the Southwest in 1938. The Santa Clara River Valley's oil industry was Morris Chevrolet's silver lining, and while the late 1930s were still tough times for many regions of the United States, William L. Morris Chevrolet was confident enough to take on Oldsmobile and Cadillac franchises.

War!

The 1940s came, and World War II swept the globe like the waters of the St. Francis Dam, plunging car dealers into a new kind of Great Depression. There were no cars; fuel was rationed; automobiles went without oil changes and tire repairs; industries shut down for the duration or went into armament production; and car dealers survived on their service departments

Bill Morris receives an award for 25 years of service with a Chevrolet franchise. *William L. Morris Chevrolet collection*

and body shops, patching together irreplaceable prewar cars.

"The war came along and, of course, people were waiting a year or year and a half to get a car," Chap Sr. recalls. "In many cases, the black market existed. I can remember a man who came into my father's dealership who was a used-car dealer in Bakersfield. He told my father he would buy my father's allotment for $2,000 a piece. This was at a time when the Chevrolet sedan had a list price of [only half that]. Being

William L. Morris Chevrolet's used-car lot before World War II. As the clouds of war loomed, Bill Morris wisely stockpiled parts and dozens of new cars. When dealerships in Los Angeles ran out of cars during the war, Morris became somewhat of a supplier. *William L. Morris Chevrolet collection*

69

offered twice the retail price would have been tempting to a lot of people, but my father's comment was, 'I didn't build this business and stay in this business just to go out of business. I built it for my sons and my sons' sons.' When people ordered a car, my father required a $25 deposit, and they put your name on the list. He had a list of all the people who had ordered cars, and he had a list of all the cars he had received. You could match your name against the cars as they came in. When you purchased the car, he sold it to you at the regular price, and he gave you a dollar to take a legal option on the car, so that if at any time in the following year, you tried to sell the car, he had the legal right to buy the car back for the dollar. He did this to keep people from going to the used-car dealers and bootleggers for quick profits. He said, 'I could do that, too, but my business was not built on that reputation.'"

The world was abuzz with predictions for World War II's outcome. Bill Morris' business wisdom surfaced again, as Chap Sr. explains.

"In 1942, the feeling among a lot of people, including car dealers, was that when the United States enters the war with the little island called Japan, the war wouldn't last long. Some of them sold their entire inventories [for some quick money], planning to take time off until the war was over. My father bought the inventories of a couple of dealers. Before too long, he had about 250 new cars in stock. My father

took his inventory and turned it over to the government. We had a warehouse, and the government told him how to preserve them. We set them on two-by-six blocks and deflated the tires to about 20 pounds of air pressure in them. They drained the motor oil. The only people they would sell a car to were people who had an OPA sticker—an allocation under the government price controls, like utility companies. For this, the government gave the cars an appreciation of something like two percent for the storage. Most of the time during the war, people who were qualified to buy a car went to Los Angeles because no one expected to be able to find cars in a little place like Fillmore, but L.A. eventually ran out of cars, and my father was the only one left with a supply. Finally, in 1945, he sold the last of those cars to, I believe, someone from the telephone company."

The war ended and a car-hungry public lined up at the dealers waiting for their numbers to come up, desperate to replace their worn-out, badly maintained vehicles. But wartime consequences still nagged at the dealers.

"Many of the cars you found on the lots right after the war, from 1946 right on up through about 1950, were loaded with accessories," Chap Sr. remembers. "The factory had their list price for the cars, but when the dealers got so many cars, they also got so many sets of seat covers, so many sets of bumper guards, so many sunshields—all these accessories. If you didn't put them on the car [and charge the customer for them], you built up an enormous stockpile of them in your parts department, so you were forced to add some of those accessories to the cars."

Postwar—The Car Years
After World War II, William L. Morris Chevrolet blossomed along with the rest of America, and the dealership's Oldsmobile and Cadillac franchises continued, and added to, the enrichment they offered the buyers of the Santa Clara Valley.

Bill Morris with grandson Chap Morris Jr. in 1994.

Chap Sr. has fond memories for the 1950s and 1960s, when every fall's announcement meant new models were unloaded in the middle of the night, showrooms were closed to the public, and public suspense was high.

"We would tape off our windows about a week in advance and hang our banners," Chap Sr. smiles. "We had our entire sales force working on displays, and the service department working on the new cars, getting them ready to sell, but we kept them hidden. Then, show day! The crowds would come in—not necessarily buyers, but many people who were curious and excited about the new things that were happening. We had drawings. The salesmen would start about seven in the morning with a kickoff breakfast, and you would work the crowd like a weasel. You'd work your way through the crowd until you found an interested buyer and sold him a car."

Nineteen fifty-five was especially exciting for Chevrolet, the Morrises, and all of America as the Big Three brought out fresh new models simultaneously. Chevrolet's theme for 1955 was "the Hot Ones."

"The last year we had a six-only was 1954, and we were losing market quickly to Ford because they had a V-8, and they emphasized power and speed, which was what the public wanted. In '55, Chevrolet came out with the 265 V-8. Fillmore was a town of about 4,000 people, and we must have had 2,000 people in over the weekend. We had a Bel Air four-door demonstrator. We put over 200 miles on the car in one day driving a mile and a half out of town and back. People were lined up to ride in it. After the presentation in the showroom, you took them out and let them drive it, and when you punched it, it moved, and you could see the stars in their eyes. When you got back to the dealership, we showed them the features album with the different colors available, and it sold itself. That was a great announcement day. We had all types of giveaways—yard sticks, bottle openers, balloons, refreshments for the crowd—and an exciting new product. The public was ready for that."

New vistas were opening up for the public as the 1950s grew late. An economy-car buyer

Chevrolet dealerships could obtain an official Chevrolet Joltmeter, an apparatus that counted the bumps delivered to the spines of passengers over a measured course. The Chevrolet salesman of the 1930s could scientifically prove that Chevrolet's Knee-Action suspension rode more smoothly and delivered fewer uncomfortable shocks than a customer's trade-in. *Marc Mirabile*

would pick a low-priced car and customize it with luxurious convenience items from the automaker's options list. By 1958, Chrysler's entry-level Plymouth could be bought in the flashy, plush, high-performance Fury option. Ford loyalists had the new and opulent Edsel within the grasp of the average-income buyer. Chevrolet's luxury car for 1958 was the new Impala, flash and dash with power and plush. More options meant more experiments, experiments that didn't always work for the dealers, as Chap Sr., explains.

"Later on, Chevrolet repeated the same sort of mistake [they had made with] Knee-Action when they introduced a pneumatic ride, which was true air suspension. In 1958, they called it Level-Air, and it was styled after the air suspension used in big freight trucks, and it leveled the car automatically and gave a car the smoothest ride possible. However,

there were product problems with it, and as it sat overnight the air would leak out of it. I went to a meeting, and I was so enthused with Level-Air that I told all my friends this was the only thing to have—a real breakthrough—and my friends believed me and bought it. I sold one to a lady who worked the night shift at the telephone office, and every morning as I went to work I'd see her car leaning to the left side. The next day it would be leaning on the right side, and the next day it would be sagging in the front or the back. We took them off a lot of cars."

Not all experiments failed. The successful ones cemented Chap Sr.'s affection for the Corvair in the 1960s.

"We had a lot of new things coming along at that time, and a lot of people wanted to be the first one on their block with something new. We had a farmer out here who had a field that was mud, and he used to let me take the customers out there and drive through that field of mud in a Corvair that you wouldn't want to drive through with a four-wheel drive. It was amazing. It would land in the mud and kind of scoot along on its belly like an alligator. I used to take people through the riverbed with it. The economy was good, and they came out with a turbo, and you could top the steep grade between here and Bakersfield for a reasonable price. It had a sports feel to it. It was a good-looking car. The Corvair convertible was a great car for someone whose son or daughter was going off to college."

Chap Sr. goes on to say that, as the gas crunch gripped the auto industry in the early 1970s, many Chevrolet dealers were wishing they had the Corvair, instead of the troublesome Vega, to combat the growing foreign car market.

William L. Morris Chevrolet has been one of Ventura County, California's, constants. It survived the Great Depression, several wars, shortages, foreign proliferation, and a devastating earthquake in 1994 that destroyed its original building and forced construction of a new modern building fronting Highway 126. At the new location, the dealership opened a morning coffee shop called Mr. Goodlunch. The coffee shop was so successful that when a talented Italian chef was thrown out of work by the closing of a fine restaurant in Santa Paula, he simply made a deal with the adaptable Morrises. William L. Morris Chevrolet, a small-town, family-owned car dealership, now serves hearty breakfasts in the morning and the fine Italian food of Chef Franco Onorato in the evenings. The smells of fine garlic and delicate spices whirl around the red and white checkered tablecloths scattered among the new cars on the showroom floor.

"The things I've loved the most have been this business and family love," William L. Morris said. "I've raised my children up in the dealership, and they've done the things I did. I think of those things at one or two o'clock in the morning. Whenever you cheat, it becomes a very uninteresting game, so we don't try to."

Morris passed away in 1994.

The men of the Morris family today carry on the legacy of their patriarch: Chap Morris Sr. (seated), Chap Morris Jr. (left), and Bill Morris (right). *Marc Mirabile*

Cox Chevrolet

Right: Cox Motor Company's used-car lot, circa 1940. Prewar views of the company's trade-in lots lack any clues that Cox participated in the OK Used Cars program. This seems to indicate that involvement in the program may have been optional or that Cox hadn't invested in the OK Used Cars adornment up to that time. *Cox Motor Company collection*

Left: Salesman Earl "Swede" Aronson officiates the 1957 Chevrolet announcement day at Cox Motor Company. The older citizens gravitated toward a poster of the new model's features while the young men gathered around the car's engine compartment. *Cox Motor Company collection*

Right: While many Chevrolet dealerships had skilled, well-staffed service departments, many a man still maintained his own car under the tree in his backyard. The Cox parts and accessory store served this type of car owner as well and sold everything from chrome trim to mirrors to accessory spotlights. The wall decorations speak directly to the serious automobile owners, urging them to pay attention to things like the clutches, brakes, and wheel alignment. *Cox Motor Company collection*

WHITNEY'S CHEVROLET—MONTESANO, WASHINGTON

A Century of Car Sales at Pioneer and First

On the side of Montesano stands a two-story building that takes up nearly the whole block. Early in the twentieth century, a Mr. Kellerman owned a jewelry store on the ground floor. Some of the customers who came in to pick out wedding rings may have been couples who had met and fallen in love at the dance hall Kellerman operated in the building's upper floor.

"Kellerman was getting by, but he was looking for a little extra income," says Forest Kelsey, who worked in the building from 1927 to 1998. "One day, someone got talking to Kellerman about automobiles, and he bought three E.M.F. cars—one for himself, and he sold the other two. Those were the only cars he ever sold. This was about 1909."

E-M-F (Everett, Metzger, and Flanders) was later taken over by its distributor, Studebaker, but it helped put the car bug in the air in pre–World War I Montesano, and the Davidson brothers opened their Buick, Chevrolet, and GMC truck dealership in the former dance hall in 1915.

Vinal Whitney was born in 1898 and was known by the initials V.I. He went to work for the Davidson brothers in 1918. A gas station was established on the premises that same year. It would become a Shell station in the 1920s.

In the fall of 1922, V.I. Whitney, then 23 years old, and his partner Ed Engen borrowed $5,000 and bought out the Davidson brothers, who moved on to another location to sell Willys-Knight. The hours were long in the 1920s, and Whitney's wife, Ruth, worked in the front office.

They didn't like the look of the sky. And where they were, it could only mean one thing. Timbers weighing tons were the ships' spines and ribs, and sails and ropes were their flesh and sinew. To the southern Atlantic Ocean, the ships were toothpicks and lint, and the men were even less.

In 1792, there was no Panama Canal. Ships from Massachusetts had to sail the Cape Horn to get to the otter pelts waiting for them on the West Coast. Storms were the Horn's hired bullies, and they screamed at, beat, and hopelessly destroyed the ships.

The ships found each other again at Nootka Island. One of the ships went clear to China and returned. Mission completed, the ships parted company, and Captain Robert Gray sailed south for a detailed exploration of the coastline, where he discovered two things: a bay safe enough and calm enough to be called a harbor, and a wide, impressive river that he successfully penetrated with his ship for roughly 25 miles. Gray described the harbor for future navigators as being watched over by a lone tree—a spruce that could be seen for miles. Twenty years before Lewis and Clark, Gray named the river after his ship, the Columbia.

For the next 90 years, the Lone Tree guided sailors to Grays Harbor, but two men came from the other direction—newspaper men from Tacoma named J. E. Calder and J. W. Walsh. Six years before Washington became a state, Calder and Walsh founded a newspaper in the town of Montesano, the westernmost newspaper in America in 1885. They named the paper The Vidette after a military term for "distant outpost." Its first issue had a circulation of 480 copies. After only a year or so, Calder moved on to the real estate business, leaving behind a newspaper surviving into the twenty-first century.

By the 1930s, Calder was very wealthy and had been elected mayor of Montesano. The town was abuzz with news that it would briefly host a distinguished visitor. The president of the United States, Franklin Roosevelt, coasted to a stop in his limousine in front of the Montesano post office.

The mayor approached the president and spoke up for the crowd to hear.

"I am welcoming you as the mayor of Montesano, Mr. President," Calder said as he handed the chief executive a wooden souvenir paperweight. Mayor Calder explained that it was made from the wood of the then-deceased Lone Tree that Captain Gray had seen in his discovery of the natural harbor that gave birth to the region's settlement.

"I appreciate this, Mr. Mayor."

Smiling, Mayor Calder said, "We'll always welcome you here, Mr. President."

From across the street, employees of a 30-year-old business watched their mayor hand the president a piece of their history. A seedling from the Lone Tree still grows at the State Capitol Museum in Olympia, Washington, and the business that witnessed the presidential visit still faces the Montesano post office—Whitney's, where cars of one kind or another have been sold and serviced since 1909.

Forest Kelsey was working for a Dodge Brothers dealership in Aberdeen, but the exuberant young man lost his driver's license for the repeated sin of speeding. As a result, he had to get a job in his hometown of Montesano. In 1927, at the age of 23, he landed a job with Whitney's Inc.

"Mr. Whitney was a fine gentleman," Kelsey recalls. "He was very religious, and he had lots of get-up-and-go. He was very aggressive—willing to take too much of a chance at times, I thought. He would borrow money, if he could get it, to improve the dealership."

Whitney was a confident risk taker, and he borrowed every penny of the $18,000 it took to expand the service station in 1928. He cut away an entire corner of the ground floor and placed the gas pumps nearly inside the building to get customers and attendants out of the sometimes constant rain.

By this time, Whitney's Inc. was selling Chevrolet, Oakland, Pontiac, and GMC trucks, but Kelsey's fondest memories revolve around the Oaklands.

"Oaklands were in a different class. An Oakland sold for about $1,600, versus eight or nine hundred for a Chevrolet, so you had to be in the money to drive one of those rascals. They were quite popular. Oaklands were large, and they had motometers, wind wings, and all that

The Whitney's sales force in the fall of 1956, posing with a just-introduced 1957 model. (L–R) Forest Kelsey, Jim Hamby, Bernie Och, Chuck Karjala, Tom Hopper, and a 20-year-old Les Foss. *Les Foss collection*

Whitney's Chevrolet-Oldsmobile in Montesano, Washington. Cars of one kind or another have been sold from this building since 1909. *Les Foss collection*

stuff that was the rage at the time. They were nice cars to drive. Now, when we had Oakland, Pontiac, and Chevrolet, they competed with each other, so we finally dropped Pontiac and picked up Oldsmobile in 1933."

The Great Depression did not come crashing down on Montesano, or much of the West, the way it had in the East's industrial cities.

"We were pretty well known by the time the Depression hit," Kelsey recalls. "An awful lot of dealers went out of business, and that accelerated our business. Mr. Whitney was a very aggressive owner, and we worked on borrowed

money completely. The whole situation wasn't as bad as it sounds, mainly because the logging continued on about an 80 percent basis."

Kelsey's modesty doesn't hide the fact that Whitney's would have gone the way of the Depression's other automotive victims if it hadn't been for his and Whitney's foresight, creativity, and effort. Kelsey reveals the secrets behind the dealership's survival of the Thirsty Thirties:

"Nineteen thirty-six was the year they paid the soldiers their bonuses for World War I. The bonus was kind of a rumor for a couple of months, and Congress decided to go ahead

with it finally. The bonuses depended on a soldier's time and service, but most of the bonuses were for about $1,500, and cars were selling for about $1,000."

Kelsey came up with a plan to commit the soldiers to buying cars through a down payment and an installment plan for the balance that would begin when the soldiers got their bonuses. Whitney found out about Kelsey's project.

Even though it was eventually successful, it was very risky. Mr. Whitney came to me one time after having been at the

A Mr. Kellerman once owned this building. A dance hall resided on the top floor and a jewelry store on the bottom one. Eventually, Mr. Kellerman sold a few E-M-F cars from this location. By the mid-1910s, the building housed the L. C. Davidson Garage and its small Buick and GMC truck franchises. *Polson Museum collection*

bank trying to borrow more money, and he said, 'Forest, what's this I hear about you taking $125 down and a note for the balance when the bonus comes through?' I said, 'Sure, that's what I'm doing,' because I thought I was doing one hell of a good job. Mr. Whitney said, 'You know if that bonus doesn't come through, we're broke.' That kind of startled me, and I told him I'd stop. He told me there was no need to stop because we were already so far into this thing that if the bonus didn't come through, we were already broke. This was in July, and their bonuses did finally came through in October. We had the biggest year in our history—499 new cars—and only one buyer failed to come up with the money, so it was a huge success.

Whitney's 1936 sales record stood until 1978.

Changing Times and Changing Thinking

"Generation gap" is usually a term associated with the 1960s. The decade's young people felt they were misunderstood by older folks because the world was changing so quickly. But more accurately, the kids in the 1960s were talking to older generations who had seen the world change much more quickly. In the 1930s, for example, a man of 60 would have been born in the 1870s, and life for him was something like

By 1918, the Davidson enterprise sold Chevrolets. Clyde Davidson poses with a Chevrolet 490 while parts manager Paul Cummings relaxes against his parts counter. *Les Foss collection*

waking up in the Old West and being in the jet-age by dinnertime. Car dealers knew there was no shortage of people who wondered, in all honesty, what a car would do that their horse couldn't.

"Many people thought cars were very dangerous instruments," Kelsey recalls, "but of course, the younger people thought cars were great because they went faster than horses. There was quite a division between those who were interested in cars and those who weren't. It was a very exciting time. When somebody got a new car, everybody knew about it."

Kelsey tangled with the old school of thought from time to time.

"We had one farmer in the '30s who was a very good customer but terribly hard to deal with. He intimated to me that he would buy a car if he could get rid of a horse. Well, heck, it was a lead! So I went out to his farm. I knew nothing about horses. It was in a stall in the barn. He said, 'If you'll give me $125 on that horse toward a car, I'll take it.' I told him I'd be back, and I went to another farmer and told him about this horse. This other farmer knew the horse and told me it was lame and that [the first farmer] knew it and wanted to get rid of it. [The second farmer] told me he'd take the horse off my hands [after the car deal] because there was nothing wrong with the horse's hoof except a bad shoe nail. I went out the next day and [made the horse-for-car deal with the first farmer], but I couldn't just bring the horse to

the dealership, so I left it in his barn. I delivered the car in two or three days, and when I went out to pick up the horse, the farmer told me, 'You have to pay me five dollars a day for feeding that horse of yours.' So he picked up $15 on me. I took the horse to the [second] farmer who was going to buy it, and two or three months later, he called me saying he wanted to show me something. I drove right out because I thought he wanted to buy a car. He had this horse there and another one just like it—*big* horses, about 1,800 pounds each—and he told me, 'There's the best team in all of Gray's Harbor County, and you can tell [the first farmer] about it. I think he ought to know.' I did tell the [first] farmer, but I don't think I made any friends!"

The 1940s came. Kelsey says word was out a year and a half in advance that the United States would eventually join the war in Europe, and people knew obtaining cars would be impossible. The citizens of Montesano were eager to get new cars before Detroit stopped making them. As predicted, the Japanese attacked Pearl Harbor, and the cars stopped coming. Kelsey spent World War II in the U.S. Army while the dealership survived on the work the service department could bring in.

The war passed, and a car-hungry public stampeded to the dealerships for the long-awaited 1946 models, opening the door to all sorts of nefarious scheming between the car dealers and the public. Whitney's had a far-reaching reputation for integrity, and Kelsey remembers the dealership selling scads of cars to customers from as far away as Seattle, more than 100 miles to the north.

"We were a very honest dealership," Kelsey says about the immediate postwar years. "We took names as people placed orders for cars, and we delivered the cars in the same order. This one gentleman came in on foot. He lived five miles out in the country, and—gee!—he just *had* to have a car. When his car came in, we called him, and we didn't tack anything on like most dealers were doing. Oh, he was so glad, and he came in with cash and shook hands with us. Three days later, I saw the car driving down the

deciding he wanted to be in the sales end of the business. In April 1956, at the age of 20, he began selling cars and started to employ the unique practices of the car business.

Technology was changing in the 1950s, and even economy-car buyers looked for luxury touches on their cars. Convenience options filtered down to the economy class, bringing new products and challenges for the young Foss.

The Powerglide [automatic transmission] came out in 1950 on Chevrolets, and I think most people were disappointed with them. The first reaction I remember was in a coffee shop when a man was asked if he had an automatic in his new Chevy, and he said he thought automatics were a good idea, but he'd be damned if he was going to pay the $175 extra for one. The

The Davidson Chevrolet service department in the early 1920s. *Polson Museum collection*

road with someone else in it. He had made himself three or four hundred dollars on the sale. There was a lot of that."

Forest Kelsey began to buy into the business in 1940, and by 1950 had acquired a 30 percent interest. V.I. Whitney, meanwhile, ran an Oldsmobile dealership in Aberdeen, where he also dealt in Firestone and General tires.

The '50s Generation Takes Root

Another player entered Whitney's story as a teenager needing a part-time job. Les Foss was born in 1936 and went to work at Whitney's as an evening service station attendant in 1951. In three years, he worked his way up from 75 cents to $1.10 per hour. Foss got an offer from a Chrysler-Plymouth dealer to work for $1.25 per hour. Kelsey said they couldn't afford that, but they could give Foss a 2 percent commission on the sale of tires. After working for a couple of other companies, Foss came back to Whitney's,

V. I. Whitney and his partner, Ed Engen, bought this business from the Davidson brothers in 1922 and added Oakland to the dealership's lineup. Whitney is seen here with a 1928 Oakland. *Les Foss collection*

Powerglide really didn't have any performance to it until 1953 when they put the valve body in it so it would start off in low and shift automatically. A lot more young people started buying them after that, but they still didn't sell really well until 1955 and after, when the 265 [V-8] came along, and there was a lot more power to operate the automatic.

The year 1955 is remembered as the year the Big Three all changed at once. Chrysler broke its stodgy styling with the beautiful new "100-Million Dollar Look." Ford Motor Company's models were all fresh and modern with the new Fairlanes, beautifully styled Victorias,

muscular Mercurys, and race-proven Lincolns. Foss remembers a lot of public fervor, but the car business took some short, hard, nervous turns as the era unfolded.

"I don't remember 1955 as well as I remember 1957, and what I remember about '57 was how disappointed all the Chevrolet dealers were because Ford was a brand-new bigger, lower, wider car. Plymouth was even lower, longer, and wider. The '57 Chevy, on the other hand, was a warmed-over '55."

Foss says the dealers were a lot happier with the 1958 Chevrolets.

"The '58 Chevy was a much more comfortable car—better riding. We were disappointed again in 1959 when they came out with the

gull-wing models. I liked the '59s, but they were not one of our better sellers. A lot of people thought the Chevys were getting too big. I had worked in the dealership long enough by then to have a good rapport with the older customers, and they didn't like the '59. They liked the 1960 models better, even though they weren't all that different, but they were toned-down, less radical."

Dealerships were able to successfully sell a number of add-on options, but Washington's wet weather and cool temperatures made air-conditioning a rarely ordered perk.

"The first Chevrolet Whitney's ever sold with air-conditioning was a '57 model," Foss remembers. "The man who ordered cars [for the dealership] thought he was ordering a deluxe heater, but he put the 'X' in the wrong box. I remember how unhappy Kelsey was when he returned from vacation and found the car had been ordered with air-conditioning. We made a demonstrator out of it, and we eventually sold it."

Whitney's first recipient of air conditioning, a Sierra Bronze and beige '57 Bel Air four-door, was still running around southwestern Washington well into the 1990s as a young dental assistant's daily form of transportation.

The Multiple Models of the 1960s
The 1960s were an exciting time for Les Foss to be in the car business. He enthusiastically recalls his experience with the Chevrolet's new multi-model lineup.

"I can't speak for other dealers, but at Whitney's we kind of liked the Corvair, except that it was awfully small," Foss remembers of Chevrolet's much-maligned entry into the compact car market. "The Ford Falcon outsold it by about two-to-one because, we thought, the Falcon was a more conventional car, and people might have been a little afraid of something different like the rear engine. My favorite demonstrator of all time was the '64 Corvair Monza Spyder with the four-carburetor engine and four-speed. It was nimble and quick. It didn't have any room in the back seat, but it was everything else a car should be."

While the Corvair was taking aim at Volk-owagen's market, the quickly conceived Chevy II was introduced in the 1962 model year to compete more directly with the Falcon and Chrysler's Valiant, which was not yet technically part of the Plymouth division.

"I've often wondered how Chevrolet got the Chevy II to market so soon, because the Falcon and Corvair had only been out two years," Foss ponders. "The Chevy II was really a very basic, straightforward car like the Falcon was. These days, it would take five or six years to develop a car like that. The Chevy II was a good seller for us, and the Malibu [in 1964] was even better. The Chevelle filled a niche for the ladies who didn't want that great big Impala but found the Chevy II didn't have enough room."

The post–World War II baby boom dumped a lot of new customers on the American car companies in the late 1960s. And while more customers were good news for the dealers, the tastes and needs of this generation made the car companies jockey for position without a crystal ball to see where their actions would take them. Some criticize this period for throwing new models at the public, seemingly without much of a plan.

"I think most people were glad to have the selection," Foss contends. "You have to remember there weren't hardly any imported cars at that time. It was nice to be able to sell people cars that were right for them as individuals."

The late 1960s also taught Foss some of the same lessons Forest Kelsey had learned in the 1930s.

I remember selling a car to a retired gentleman one day who thought that, in his advanced years, he should have an automatic

Forest Kelsey went to work for Whitney's in 1927. He is seen here recapping, or regrooving, a tire in the service department's tire room and filling the gas tank on the company tow truck. The driver of the tow truck was Whitney's employee Curt Hansen, who became the general manager of Whitney's Oldsmobile in the neighboring city of Aberdeen, Washington, and later had his own Olds franchise in Centralia, Washington. *Les Foss collection*

Whitney's service department in 1928. Curt Hansen works at the bench on the left. Rea Kellerman pulls a chainfall while Morris Simpson (right) watches. *Les Foss collection*

I can remember taking in an Olds 98 on an Olds Omega, and a year later the same customer wanted a 98 again. They wanted smaller cars until they had them; then they wanted their big cars back. We had people trading Monte Carlos in for Vegas, and they were disappointed in the size and performance. They went from a V-8 to a four-cylinder, and the gas mileage wasn't even all that much better in those days. It was better, but not better enough to compensate for the loss of comfort and convenience."

Foss agrees there were a few troublesome Chevrolet vehicles, but most problems were manageable.

"The early Corvairs had the problem of throwing the fan belts. A deeper pulley took care of most of that. The Vega engine in the '70s was far worse. [In about 1980] I had a conversation with Jim Hamby, one of the longtime salesmen, and he said, 'In the '60s, we had to live down the Covair, in the '70s, we had to live down the Vega, and now, we have to live down the diesel.'"

transmission, which he had never owned before. We had this little '61 Mercury Comet on the used-car lot. Somebody had told the gentleman he should drive with his left foot on the brake and his right foot on the throttle. As we were driving around town on the test drive, he would come down on the brake pedal like he was coming down on a clutch. He put me into the dashboard four times! Finally, I just braced my hands against the dash and said, 'Let's go.' I can also remember people who absolutely refused to buy power steering, and some people didn't like automatic transmissions because they felt they wasted gas.

Whitney passed away in the late 1960s and left the business in Kelsey's capable hands. Kelsey took the dealership through the tough times of the 1970s, beginning with the fuel crisis of 1973 and 1974.

"We had lines at our gas station," Foss remembers. "People suddenly wanted smaller cars.

Glen Taylor in the Whitney's lube room in 1937. *Les Foss collection*

Whitney Chevrolet, July 1942. *Les Foss collection*

Kelsey sold the business in 1980 to longtime Whitney's salesman Stormy Glick, who has taken the dealership into the twenty-first century. Still, Kelsey visited the dealership daily well into his nineties.

Kelsey passed away in 2002. He once said, "Ever since coming down from Canada as a small boy of three years old, cars have always fascinated me. I've been fortunate to do exactly what I've wanted to do all of my life."

Whitney's "Daylight Service Department" in 1948. The extra light the building allowed in was helpful to the mechanics. However, in the summer, the glass roof acted just like a greenhouse. Eventually it had to be covered. *Les Foss collection*

Ferman Chevrolet

W. F. Ferman was in the bicycle business before he moved on to more powerful machines. After the battleship *Maine* exploded in Havana, Cuba, the Tampa Cycle Company displayed its business acumen by adding typewriters and cameras to its merchandise. The enterprise took on Oldsmobile in 1902 and Cadillac in 1903. In 1914, Ferman took on technologically advanced Dodge Brothers' products and acted as the distributor for eight western-Florida counties. As the Great Depression sunk its teeth into Tampa, the Ferman business very briefly added DeSoto and Packard to its product offerings. In 1930, Fred Ferman Sr. took on a new franchise and Ferman Chevrolet came into existence, seen here at its Jackson Street location in the late 1930s. *Ferman Chevrolet collection*

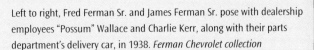

The Ferman Chevrolet accessory counter in the 1940s. A stack of new DeLuxe seat covers are waiting to be put away. DeLuxe Radios are on sale for $59, and Custom DeLuxe Radios are priced at $79. The counter also offers a variety of replacement taillights for various years of Chevrolet and a roadside emergency light. The far-left corner reveals an elaborate touch-up paint selector, a Delco battery display, and replacement floor mats, while the far right displays Burex gasoline filters, a GM tissue dispenser, replacement truck mirrors for $17.95, and what could be "truck vents" for $19.95. Along the right wall, chrome accessory wheel covers, exhaust deflectors, and other small goodies await buyers. A sign on the back wall warns, "Prices shown do not include installation." *Ferman Chevrolet collection*

Left to right, Fred Ferman Sr. and James Ferman Sr. pose with dealership employees "Possum" Wallace and Charlie Kerr, along with their parts department's delivery car, in 1938. *Ferman Chevrolet collection*

When it came to sick cars, the Ferman Chevrolet service department was always just what the doctor ordered. GM's art department's influence is seen here. In the background rest a classic Sun Motor Tester, a Sun distributor machine, and a cabinet-equipped workbench marked "Sun Scientific Analysis." The Vega kept many Chevrolet service departments busy during the gas crunch of the early 1970s. This Vega, ironically billed as "the little car that does everything well," gets its performance checked with an AC Diagnostic Tune-Up Center machine. Note the Chevrolet logo on the clock located high in the stairwell. *Ferman Chevrolet collection*

The 1956 announcement day at Ferman Chevrolet. *Ferman Chevrolet collection*

NO FOOLIN'··· IT'S FERMAN'S FABULOUS UNVEILING SALE!

FEATURING FACTORY FRESH 1956 CHEVROLETS FOR AS LITTLE AS $1595 FULL PRICE delivered at Ferman's IN TAMPA!

● It's true! It's fantastic! Pay only $1595 for this spankin' new, factory-fresh '56 Chevrolet— a full 6 passenger, 6 cylinder, beautifully chromed 2-door, standard-equipped model 1502 sedan, factory-guaranteed by Tampa's oldest and largest bona-fide new car dealer. Yes, Ferman continues the '55 "public service" sales policy into '56 models. As before, absolutely no bargain sales to curbstone peddlers for their resale. All these spectacular savings are reserved for YOU—the motoring public! Trades? Yes, sir! The usual considerate terms and convenient arrangements. See the new '56 Chevrolet today, in our newly expanded display showrooms!

CHEVROLET'S "GOT IT" IN '56—and you can get it at fabulous savings, now, at

FERMAN CHEVROLET

OPEN WEEKDAYS 8 A.M. - 9 P.M., SUNDAYS NOON 'TIL 6 P.M. 407 JACKSON

85

WEBSTER MOTORS—CODY, WYOMING

Bud, Bill, and Other Pioneers

"I was born on a ranch on the Graybull River near Meeteetse, Wyoming, in 1912," Bud Webster tells. "It was a sheep and cattle ranch 28 miles from Cody. My dad ran quite a few head of cattle, and several bands of sheep. A band of sheep is about 1,500 head. It wasn't unusual for me to ride about 50 miles a day. Later on, I was put in charge of the sheep in the wilderness area. We had three bands of sheep up there, and I had to pack in on horseback. I did that for about five years, and then I graduated from the University of Wyoming and went off seek my fortune."

Bud Webster is part cowboy, part academic, part Old West, and part modern businessman. People raised in ranching often have a hyper-practical acceptance of reality. They accept facts quickly. The rain must fall, or the crop will die. The sick bull must be put down quickly, or the disease will spread. When reality throws bad weather or bad times at a rancher, he or she accepts it and deals with it. This is the directness that helped tame the West in the nineteenth century, and it's the same directness that turned to face the exciting, growing auto industry in the early twentieth century. Bud Webster backed his pragmatic approach up with an education.

I entered the University of Wyoming in 1931, and I took all the accounting and business administration [classes] I could," Webster recalls. "I was not a stellar student by any means. I always said I should have gotten my degree from the campus shop instead of the college of business. I did enjoy the University of Wyoming, but 1935 was a very, very difficult time, and that's when I graduated. You couldn't buy a job. So I got a job in Los Angeles, California, with the Richfield Oil Corporation for $81.50 a month. I had applied for a job with the Wyoming State Board of Equalization, and after nine or ten months with Richfield, in the spring of 1936, I was offered this job with the Board of Equalization as a field officer. A year later, in 1937, I audited the Chevrolet dealership here in Cody and determined they were bankrupt. My brother had just sold his interest in the ranch, and he had some money. I sold my 1936 Ford for $400 and was able to raise $600 out of my savings, so I had $1,000 and my brother had the rest. We went to Great Falls [Montana] and applied for the Chevrolet dealership in Cody, and they gave it to us. They determined because of my background in business administration and accounting classes that I should sign Paragraph Three, so in October of 1937, I signed the contract with Chevrolet, and I still have it. We went into business at the edge of the 1938 recession. Now back in 1936, the Franklin Roosevelt reelection

You Can Do Better With Webster

C. E. WEBSTER
Manager

Top: The citizens of Cody, Wyoming, could "do better with Webster" after Bud Webster bought the city's failing Chevrolet franchise in 1937. Webster has taken the dealership into the twenty-first century, and at age 90, still works six days a week. *Bud Webster collection*

Left: Bud Webster. *Bud Webster collection*

campaign theme song was 'Happy Days Are Here Again,' but in 1937 and '38, unemployment went back up to 25 percent. In 1940, I bought out my brother, who didn't care for the business, and I became the sole owner of Webster Chevrolet. Early on, we had five mechanics, a service manager, a grease monkey, a parts manager, a bookkeeper, and two salesmen.

Some Chevrolet dealers went into the business because they loved automobiles and wanted to be on the cutting edge of new and exciting events. Webster's first love was the business world. He might not have counted himself among the "gearheads" attracted to the car business by the smells of gasoline and hot metal, but Webster's business sense gave him a feel for the producers of the time.

"We had two models when I first started in '37—the Standard, which did not have Knee-Action; and the Deluxe, which did," Webster recalls. "The Deluxe with Knee-Action sold for about $850, and the Standard with the straight axle sold for about $700. Besides the Knee-Action on the Deluxes, a heater was about the only option these cars had. The Standard straight axle rode pretty rigid—not quite as soft as the Knee-Action Deluxes.

"Chevrolet had a water pump that kept malfunctioning, and sometimes it only had 20 miles on the vehicle when it needed replacing. Oftentimes, if it weren't replaced, it would fall off and go through the radiator, and that was a terrible, terrible problem. It wasn't corrected until 1938.

"In 1938, Ford still had the manual brakes. Chevrolet went into hydraulic brakes in 1936, and the sales of the Ford just plummeted. I'm sure the records will show Chevrolet outsold Ford by [a substantial margin]. Ford didn't come out with hydraulic brakes until 1939. Henry Ford said that with hydraulic brakes, if you lose one, you lose them all, whereas with manual brakes, you will have the others working. I had a 1936 Ford with manual brakes, and by god, I'll tell you, you didn't have much braking, and you had to be careful. Hydraulic brakes were a great thing for Chevrolet at that time."

As with many rural and small-town dealers in prewar America, bartering played a role at Webster Chevrolet.

"I traded for a lot of horses. The Webster Ranch is over 100 years old and still belongs to the family and is run by my nephews. I used to take horses in trade and put them on the ranch. I wasn't above trading for whatever I could, but

He must have had a home in the East. He must have been thinking about a warm hearth and a warm bed. But he wasn't there; he was here, slugging through deep snow one rugged step at a time trying to make contact like he promised. His breath must have been frozen to his beard. His old, abused moccasins must have been packing snow around his feet. And every day must have been a struggle to keep frostbite from chewing off fingers and toes. The only thing worse than the agony of frozen extremities is anticipating the warm, cozy, comfortable feeling of truly freezing to death. Better to be in living pain than dying comfort?

There was a smell in the air—a burning, rotting stench—and it was getting stronger. Did he already know the Indians called it the Stinking River? His assignment was to contact the Indians and open the doors of trade. Did he come around a bend? Did he crest a hill? Or did he see the steam rising through the trees? A hellish landscape is a comfort to a freezing man, and this place was hellish. Hot, sulfur-reeking steam shot into the air through cones of accumulated minerals, and pools of hot, stinking water bubbled in crusty craters. Nothing grew too close to the mess. It looked poisonous. And somehow it looked inviting.

Lewis and Clark had set off from St. Charles, Missouri, in 1803 in search of a continuous east-west water passage across the still new-seeming American continent. John Colter left the party before it returned to the East to establish contact and trade with the Indians. He was alone when he found one of the geyser fields Wyoming is now celebrated for, but at the time, no one believed him. They called it Colter's Hell. It simmers in the Shoshone River's canyons, which form the eastern gate to Yellowstone National Park from the rugged Big Horn Basin. The valley was rediscovered later in the nineteenth century when Colter's footsteps were followed by fur trade and cattle kings, everyone from French and German counts to, by the twentieth century, those in the mining and oil industries.

Buffalo Bill Cody was world famous for his Wild West exhibition, although he resisted calling it a "show" because he regarded it as presenting the West's realities. He was brought in as a partner to promote the new and growing Big Horn Basin—hence, the little city of Cody, Wyoming, where the Irma Hotel still stands as Buffalo Bill's tribute to his daughter.

The United States was only about 20 years old when John Colter stumbled into the Big Horn Basin, and Chevrolet's dealer network was only about 20 years old when northern Wyoming native Bud Webster bought a failing Chevrolet franchise. Webster was only 25 years old when he began his career with Chevrolet. When he reached his nineties, he was still working for the company—six days a week nonetheless.

The madam of Cody's house of ill repute had gone into the tamer nightclub business and needed some extra capital, so she offered Bud Webster this lot at the corner of Sheridan and 16th in 1948. *Bud Webster collection*

I was never a wheeler-dealer either. If I saw a horse I could take in on trade and get $50 for, which was about the going price for a good saddle horse at that time, I'd trade for it. I traded for lots of Model As. The Ford Model A was a great car. If a guy traded in a car to us and wanted to keep his gas, we'd drain his damned gas tank and give it to him."

The Great Depression had been easing through the late 1930s, but 1938 plagued the United States with another deep recession year, possibly spawned by dramatic freezing and flooding weather in the Southwest and war cries in Europe. But despite the economic downturn, rumbles from Washington, D.C., resulted in a lively showroom at Webster Chevrolet.

"In 1938, the government was considering the Townsend Plan. It was a nationwide movement promoted by this guy named Townsend who was accepting contributions from older people to try to get this bill through Congress that would pay each person over 65—men and women—$200 a month. I had people pouring in to look at new cars, anticipating being able to buy one. Of course, it was not a feasible plan and was never enacted, but the older people thought it was a great idea, and we had a lot of people in here looking at cars."

Every winter, the Wyoming winds howl and the blizzard clouds gather. By 1940, winds of war were gathering over Europe. The Japanese bombed Pearl Harbor, the United States joined

World War II, and the cars stopped coming to the dealerships.

"I never applied for deferment [from the draft], but I was married, and I was in this business, and they gave it to me," Webster recalls. "I was never involved in the war, and that's a sad deal, but that's the way it was. Starting in 1941, I bought all the cars I could get from General Motors, and I really got a tremendous number of vehicles, including a lot of trucks. General Motors came up with the Sloan Plan [named for Alfred P. Sloan, the head of GM at the time]. There were dealers who were ready to throw in the towel, saying [about the anticipated war] 'This is the end.' The dealers were discouraged and wanted to get out of the business. Sloan

came out with this plan whereby the dealers would receive the same percentages of vehicles they received in 1941 when production resumed after the war, and I believe that went on for two years. Production stopped on April 1, 1942. I had bought all the vehicles I could afford from dealers who wanted to go out of the business, so I had a very high percentage. If I remember right, the sample was taken from January 1, 1941, to March of 1942, and after the war, I received the same percentage of Chevrolet's total production that I had received during that sample period."

Webster's business sense gave him the confidence to take certain risks.

I also bought Fords, Studebakers, and 20 International trucks [to get me through the war]. I gave a check to International for $64,000 for the trucks, thinking General Motors would floor plan them [meaning they would finance the showroom inventory for the dealer], but GM refused. They said their policy was to floor plan only General Motors products and, even then, only to a certain degree. We had a local individual who had a finance company, and he was really a great guy and a good friend of mine. I went up to see him and said, 'Tom, I've written this check for $64,000 and, of course, I don't have any money, and now GM won't floor plan them.' He said to his secretary, 'Write him out a check, Ida.' We knew we were going to need a lot of tires [if the war started], and I went out and bought out all the tires I could buy. Most people couldn't sell them, but I [was authorized by the government as a dealer] to buy them for resale. Tires were rationed, and you couldn't sell them unless you had a certificate. I bought thousands and thousands of dollars worth of tires, great numbers of them. I bought all the tires that Billings Hardware had for sale, about 100 of them, including some 24-inch tires [for old cars], and I sold them

Webster Chevrolet in the 1990s. *Bud Webster collection*

all during the war. People who had certificates to sell tires [couldn't find any to sell], so of course, we sold tires to them. It was a source of tremendous income during the war. I tried to keep all the paperwork straight so I could show everything was legal, because being that I was deferred out of the war, they were looking at me. It helped me a great deal even after the war.

Times of short supply bring out the good, the bad, and the ugly in human nature, separating those who play by the rules and care about others from the characters only concerned with benefiting themselves.

"The period right after the war was a very interesting time," Webster remembers. "People wanted to get on the waiting list for new cars, but we never took a list. We kept our new vehicles in the warehouse, and if a good customer came in, he got a car, and he got it at the OPA price, but if a guy came in who hadn't dealt with me before, I'd tell him that I couldn't be sure I'd be able to deliver him a car within a year. That backed off most of them. I'd also tell them, 'Well, I bet a year from now, we'll have cars running out of our ears, so how about a deposit of $500?' That backed them all off. I never had a single taker on that deal, but I sold hundreds of cars to our good customers. There was a [high-ranking religious leader in our region] who would go around to the different dealers and introduce himself [emphasizing his position with the church], and he would tell the dealers he needed a car *oh-so* bad. He got seven cars that way and sold them all on the black market. There was a lot of that going on."

During the postwar boom, Webster's original building proved not to be large enough. This is when his lifelong connection with Park County personalities paid off.

"Cody only had about 3,000 people in it when I first started, and it was just a small dealership. I had 75 feet of Main Street. I look back at that first dealership now, and I wonder how in the hell I got by. Later on, I acquired the property of the Ford dealership, where we still are. There was a former madam of a house of ill fame in Cody by the name of Cassie. She had ceased to be the madam of the brothel in 1933 and went out and established a nightclub called Cassie's. I had met her on visits to the nightclub, and we became quite good friends, and I liked

Bud Webster began selling Chevrolets at the age of 25. Right away, he was in for a challenge. The 1937 Chevrolets kept the service department busy with chronic water pump problems. From the Tom Meleo collection.

to hear her stories. I went up to see her at the hospital one day [in the 1940s], and she was waiting for someone to take her home. I said, 'I'll take you home, Cassie,' and on the way home, she told me how hard up for money she was. She owned 125 feet at this great intersection here in Cody—the corner of Sheridan and 16th. I said, 'Well, Cassie, I'll buy your lot, but I can only pay you $20,000 for it, and I know you have better offers than that.' She said, 'Yeah, but they don't have any money.' [She decided to sell it to me], and I asked her how she wanted the money. She said, 'Tens and twenties.' I went down to the Shoshone Bank and picked up two sacks—one with a thousand ten-dollar bills and one with five-hundred twenty-dollar bills. So I had acquired this great intersection in Cody and made a used-car lot out of it. Since that time, I've acquired the whole block—the most valuable piece of commercial property in Cody by far. The city even deeded over the alley, so it's a solid block, which is very unusual. And this is our present location."

Most dealers, and certainly today's classic car enthusiasts, smile at the 1949 to 1954 model years when the jet-age took firm hold on styling and performance —offering lower bodies, fast-backs, gun-sight hood ornaments, and high performance from Oldsmobile's 303, Hudson's 308, and Chrysler's 331. There were whiz-bang names for everything GM offered—Hydra-Matic, Powerglide, Dynaflow. For Webster, it was the business cycles of the time that held his attention as he guided his dealership out of pre-war business practices and into the bold, new, high-gear postwar era.

"[Some of the dealers] would have gone broke if the war hadn't interceded. Our zone office was taken over by a [new zone manager] shortly before the war, and I'm here to tell you, any dealer who wasn't doing the job got a visit from him and the ensuing zone managers, and they literally threatened. [The zone manager went into a dealership in another Wyoming city] and he said, 'We're going to cancel you.' [The dealer] said, 'You'll have to do it the hard way.' That's the way it was in those days. They could

cancel you without cause or any recourse on the part of the dealer. They expected the dealer to have 35 percent of the market in their price class in both trucks and passenger cars. If you fell below that, you got a visit. I didn't ever get a visit because they thought I was a fair-haired boy."

The National Automobile Dealers Association, or NADA, worked to correct the power disparity between dealers and managers.

"I was NADA director for Wyoming from 1953 to 1959. A Wyoming senator, Joseph C. O'Mahoney, sponsored the Day in Court Bill. *Time* magazine wrote that O'Mahoney literally wrote the final version of that bill on the floor of the United States Senate, and it gave the dealers the right to sue if they were canceled by the factory without cause. He was very well thought of. He gave a speech at the NADA convention that lasted about a hour, and every 30 seconds, he got a standing ovation. The dealers went crazy, and the factory didn't like it. It was said that, prior to this bill, a factory mail clerk could cancel a dealer contract."

Webster didn't win every battle, though. In 1958, Congress passed the Disclosure of Automobile Information Act, forcing a vehicle's retail price to be posted right on the vehicle. The intent was to stop unscrupulous dealers from artificially padding retail prices with mysterious shipping charges and unordered options.

"[Mike] Monroney was a senator from Oklahoma who sponsored the bill for the window sticker," Webster explains. "The window sticker would be on the car like it is today with the retail price. I opposed that as best I could, along with another dealer, but we lost. Here's the problem: If the factory determines that price on the windshield, they can raise their price to the dealer, but the dealer can't raise the price to the public."

The factory could then charge the dealers more for the car without suffering any consequences. But if the dealer passed the increased price along to the customer, the customer could refuse to buy the car.

"We had a 24 percent discount, meaning if a car sold [to the public] for $2,500, our price for the car was $1,900. That is exactly what

happened. All the car manufactures have raised their prices to us over the years, and now 40 or 50 years later, we have some models where we can only make $1,500 maximum. They squeezed us because they knew we would have to post these prices, but the factory could raise their price to us, and we couldn't do anything about it. I spoke out the best I could against that. There were some dealers who thought it was a great thing, and they supported the damned thing, and it passed. I'm a practical S.O.B. if nothing else, and I knew what the factories were going to do. You'd have to be a big-volume dealer to sell the cars at the factory's window-sticker price in order to make enough money to stay in business. You also need room to bargain with people, and of course, there's no room to dicker with the factory prices in place."

Webster's are the views of a businessman. The successes of Chevrolet's prewar models and 1955's Hot Ones were taken in stride, with some disappointments in the Turboglide, Corvair, and Vega. Webster had heard William Holler say Coca-Cola was America's greatest franchise and that Chevrolet's goal should be to surpass Coke and become America's greatest brand name. When the Coca-Cola franchise for northern Wyoming became available during World War II, Webster bought it and ran it until he sold it in 1979, saying he never would have bought it if William Holler hadn't complimented Coca-Cola's practices.

"The best thing that ever happened to Bud Webster was going into business in 1937 with unemployment at 25 percent and things being tougher than hell," Webster says. "It really taught me lessons I've been thankful for ever since. Thirty-five car dealers have come and gone in this area since I became a dealer. We sell and keep punching, and that's what we've done over these last 65 years. Some of these dealers become rich, they become loose with their money, and next thing you know, they've lost their business. You see, if you go into business when times are good, you develop some bad habits. If you go into business when times are bad, you learn to be careful."

City Chevrolet

This Chevrolet franchise in Great Falls, Montana, was founded as Taylor Chevrolet by Doc Taylor. In the early 1930s, the dealership was owned by Paul Seese and sported an elaborate, one-of-a-kind Bowtie sign high above its roof. Robert Oakland bought the dealership in 1954, but City Chevrolet still honors Seese by keeping his sign mounted on the front of its present building. *City Chevrolet collection*

These "72-Car Club" winners are at the train station on their way to be honored at the annual convention in Portland, Oregon. In 1928, these dealers sold at least 72 cars. Longtime Chevrolet dealer Bud Webster of Cody, Wyoming, reports that, by the time he was in the Chevrolet business in the late 1930s, the ante had been upped to the "100-Car Club," wherein a salesman who sold 100 cars in a year won $100, or, in some years, a gold watch. Two of the men pictured, Joe Daly and John Dea, sold for Taylor Chevrolet. At the time the photo was taken, John Dea was in a heated wager with Layton Todd of a Chevrolet dealership in Bozeman, Montana, to see who could sell the most cars in the month of October. A 20-pound turkey was at stake. *City Chevrolet collection*

FELIX CHEVROLET—LOS ANGELES, CALIFORNIA

Urban Gem

If you stand at the intersection of Figueroa Street and Jefferson Boulevard in Los Angeles and look north, you'll see the giant glass towers of commerce that surround city hall—the now–little–seeming, snow-white, Art Deco pearl. Looking west, you'll spot the Shrine Auditorium's Moorish

Bill Felix emigrated from Mexico and founded Felix Chevrolet in 1922. He established a very successful dealership and was tragically killed playing polo in 1936. The dealership became the property of his widow, Ruth, who turned the day-to-day operations over to a general manager. In 1955, Ruth Felix retired, and successful used-car dealer Nick Shammas was in the right place at the right time. Shammas became the dealership's new operator.
Felix Chevrolet collection

turrets that have welcomed limousines full of movie stars to the Academy Awards on several occasions through the decades. On the southwest corner, you'll see the University of Southern California (USC), which counts George Lucas and Neil Armstrong among its alumni.

For the Chevrolet devotee, the true gem of this intersection is located on the northeast corner. This is where Felix Chevrolet's giant sign stands as a cartoon symbol of American commerce. Its pleasantly humorous image, as familiar to Los Angelinos as the Coliseum or Hollywood Sign, masks its more serious meanings. Felix the Cat took his place in the 1950s over a business that had already survived the Great Depression, the death of its founder, and shortages of World War II. The smiling feline has entered the twenty-first century watching over Nickolas Shammas, the charismatic dealer-operator who guided the record-setting enterprise through the highs, lows, and pitfalls of the giant, glittering urban dealership. Felix Chevrolet and Nick Shammas both started with humble means, but time and circumstance would eventually introduce them to each other and launch them to the top of the game.

"I started out in high school selling cars to the students and repairing them," Nick Shammas remembers. "I attended Fairfax High School in Los Angeles, and I graduated in 1937. Through high school, I sold about 22 cars, and I repaired the principal's car and the teachers' cars. I had a little garage at Beverly and Gardner while I was still in high school, and I worked at night and on weekends. From then, I went to junior college in Santa Monica, and I held down three jobs, helping support my mother and sister. It was very difficult.

"I moved on and opened up a used-car lot. I worked as a mechanic for a used-car dealer on

Nick Shammas signs on with Chevrolet as the new dealer-operator of Felix Chevrolet in 1955.
Felix Chevrolet collection

Santa Monica Boulevard named Carl Goodwin. Carl was an old sage in the car business and was considered a very, very capable person, and he taught me quite a bit about the used car business. Other than the 22 cars I sold in high school, I'd had no other experience. When I began to operate a little stronger and knew a little more, I got the finance companies around Carl Goodwin's place to consign cars to me, and then I went over onto a car lot on La Brea Street owned by Bob Lydick. Bob was the one who had the [dealer's license], but Bob didn't do quite as well himself as I did, but I got these cars on consignment, and I bought a few with the limited money I had, and I began to make money.

"About a year later, I opened a used car lot at Beverly Boulevard. I was dating my [future] wife at that time, and she told me I should get my own license rather than trying to get along with these other people, but I have to say I learned a lot working with Bob. I opened my own lot at 2384 North Pico, and later I moved it down to 4477 Pico. While I was doing this, I had a lot on the corner of Beverly and Normadie—a little-bitty one, an extra lot. So I was branching out, so to speak.

"Now, you have to remember used cars at that time were selling for 150 to 200 dollars, and we would take 15 or 20 dollars down and 5 dollars a week on the car. If you missed payment, you could leave your wristwatch, and I would wait until you came back in. The watch had value to the customer. Those were the kind of Depression days we had to live through. It was a humble beginning, but the lot on North Pico was a nice lot right across from the Sears [and] Roebuck store. From there, I learned the business."

In 1922, Bill Felix founded his Chevrolet dealership at 12th Street and Grand Avenue.

"Bill Felix was from Mexico, and he was a smart, smart man," Shammas says with undisguised admiration. "He had built the business into a top-notch operation, but he was killed—crushed tragically—playing polo in 1936. Contrary to the policy at General Motors at that time against letting a woman run a dealership, they let Ruth Felix own the dealership as long as the managers stayed in place. She wasn't in the store much, but her general manager took over for her and ran it while she continued to own the company."

Felix the Cat originated from the pen of cartoonist Otto Messmer in 1919 and was adopted by Felix Chevrolet in the 1920s. In 1958, Nick Shammas took the cheerful feline to his new place next to L.A.'s Harbor Freeway. The mascot announced to the world that Felix Chevrolet had moved to Figueroa at Jefferson, the former location of a Lincoln-Mercury dealership.

A *wealthy man moved from the antebellum South to Los Angeles (to avoid the coming conflict?) and took his favorite slave with him. Biddy Mason was a good slave. She was intelligent, resourceful, a self-taught nurse and midwife. But when her owner decided to move back home, Mason refused to go, and the courts upheld her freedom. She stayed free, invested in land, and became very wealthy.*

Hollywood doesn't reveal the real city—the Los Angeles that still inhabited the Old West into the jazz age, the Los Angeles of grape vineyards and bean fields, the Los Angeles of average people of everyday greatness.

Calle Saltamontes, or "Grasshopper Street" in English, headed south from downtown. The street's name was changed to honor an early governor of California under Mexican rule—Figueroa—and 34th Street was renamed to honor an early president of the United States—Jefferson.

In the automobile's earliest days, the roads weren't marked, and driving an unreliable, newfangled contraption through the uniquely Southwestern immensity was a frightening gamble. The Automobile Club of Southern California won the public's loyalty with a massive sign-posting operation beginning in 1907, and the red, white, and blue porcelain-coated signs still turn up in the Mojave Desert's sand washes. The Auto Club needed offices to match its success, and their beautiful Spanish-style building has stood opposite Fatty Arbuckle's former home since 1923.

A new Chevrolet turned onto the street with a license plate frame touting "Felix Chevrolet—Figueroa at Jefferson." To an Angelino, it's just called "Fig."

In the days of live commercials, Nick Shammas had boxer Joe Louis and *Highway Patrol* star Broderick Crawford on as guests. This brand of publicity timed well with a booming economy in Los Angeles, leading to what Shammas calls the dealership's "glory days." The dealership broke the million-dollar mark in 1959. In 1963, its staff of 120 salesmen sold over 23,000 new and used cars. *Felix Chevrolet collection*

By 1940, Felix Chevrolet was one of the marque's giants, but after the Japanese bombed Pearl Harbor, the cars stopped coming. The night sky in Los Angeles went black for the war, and spotters scanned the Pacific's horizon for enemy ships and planes.

"I was married by the time the war broke out, and I opened a machine shop downtown at 2010 Stanford Street in 1942," Shammas recalls. "I didn't make any money for two years, and I worked like a dog. I never worked so hard in my life. I went down to 133 pounds—just skin and bone. The war was on, and I didn't pass the draft. I had a murmuring heart. I had about 35 machines and about 50 people in there, and we worked three eight-hour shifts. I would work all day until my wife came down, and we would go to a show. After I got back, I would strip back down to my work clothes and go through the 35 machines to make sure they were running on size."

Shammas' machine shop made special prototypes for the Cal Tech engineering department's war efforts, creating some of the first

FELIX CHEVROLET SALES FORCE-FIRST ANIVERSARY 1956

The staff of Felix Chevrolet when Nick Shammas took over the business. *Felix Chevrolet collection*

fuses for bazookas and special emergency patch kits for *Liberty Ships* damaged at sea.

The war clouds eventually cleared, and the American auto industry's glamorous postwar years commenced. Nick Shammas and a partner started a used-car lot in the San Fernando Valley northwest of Los Angeles, putting him on a course that intersected with Felix Chevrolet in 1955.

"I was president of the car dealers' association out in the San Fernando Valley—an association that included both new- and used-car dealers, which was unusual—and I gave a speech at the beginning of 1953 telling what a great year it was going to be. It turned out to be a disastrous year. Nineteen fifty-three was a big drop in the used-car business, and I decided to get into the new-car business. I went out knocking on doors, and Chevrolet was happy to get me. They came out to my used car lot and saw how neat and clean it was and what an outstanding operation it was. They offered me the Felix Chevrolet franchise. They said, 'We have a franchise we're going to show you, but you can't say anything because the owner died, and it's still a sensitive subject with Mrs. Felix who now has it.' So I came down and looked at it. It was a three-story building loaded with people, and I said, 'Oh, my gosh, how am I going to run that great big thing?' Chevrolet told me not to worry and that I'd do fine. I had the money in my back pocket, but I wanted to play safe, so I borrowed the money. It took a quarter of a million dollars to start. Originally, I had started in the car business with $300 when I had a little garage on Beverly and Gardner. After I bought

One corner of the Felix Chevrolet lot in the late 1960s. *Felix Chevrolet collection*

I don't think any other sign would have withstood it. The Harbor Freeway was the whole idea behind putting the sign up. The city was absolutely adamant that I couldn't put that sign up, but Mayor [C. Norris] Poulson overrode that decision."

The move inaugurated Felix Chevrolet's golden era.

"We made something close to a million dollars in 1959, which was a tremendous amount of money at that time. We just had a spectacular operation. At our peak, we had 120 salesmen, a fabulous staff, and we were on television. Most importantly, we had built up a momentum, and we had the inventory [based on our high allocation]. We had five used-car lots with over 750 used cars available at any one time. We sold 23,000 cars in one year, new and used. That was in the year '62, '63. We enjoyed great success up until the riots in 1965. The riots really hurt us and all of L.A., but we stuck it out when many of the others all left. We kept going, thanks to the Latino people. We have a

Felix, I associated myself with some very capable people, and we became the largest automobile company in the western half of the United States. We moved to our present location in 1958, and '59 was our first real big year."

Felix the Cat was born from the pen of cartoonist Otto Messmer in 1919 and adopted by Felix Chevrolet in the 1920s. In 1958, Felix the Cat took his place next to L.A.'s Harbor Freeway and announced to the world that Felix Chevrolet had moved to, in the words of thousands of ads to come, Figueroa at Jefferson.

"The sign was created by the Heath Company," Shammas recalls. "The fellow who owned Heath was originally an aircraft engineer. The sign was made like the wing of an aircraft so it would stand the wind. We had a terrible windstorm, and it cracked the supports that were 12-by-12 wood, reinforced with steel.

Nick Shammas fronting a gala show for Chevrolet, circa 1970. *Felix Chevrolet collection*

Shammas displays his first machinist's handbook and a Chevrolet Quality Dealer Award.

good rapport in the Latino community, and we try to earn it."

America, Los Angeles, and Chevrolet were all at their peaks in the late 1950s and early 1960s. Times were good—almost too good.

"Chevrolet's biggest fear was that they would sell too many cars, and the government would spin them off [from General Motors as a monopoly]," Shammas explains. "General Motors had 57 percent of the market, and that was dangerously close to a monopoly, and they were worried. They had Ed Cole in there as their engineer, and he did marvelous things for Chevrolet product-wise, contributing to the

Corvette and other things. When I bought Felix Chevrolet and moved to this location, that was the biggest change of my life. We grew like a weed, and by '59, we were setting the sales records. Everything was in our favor. The product was hot, and we had the biggest allocation. There was Central Chevrolet downtown at Seventh Street and Central Avenue, and they were the giant. They called themselves Mighty Central Chevrolet, and they were out to drown little Nicky, but it didn't work."

General Motors and Chevrolet knew to listen to the dealers for public feedback, and Nick Shammas was one of those to whom they listened.

"I was on the forward development board of General Motors. I went to Detroit along with others from other parts of the country to advise GM as to what was happening on the firing line. I did that for about four years. They took a select number of dealers from different markets, and they would interrogate us about various aspects of merchandise, sales, and customer reactions. We spent a lot of time discussing various models and how they affected the market. One in every four cars in California at that time was a Chevrolet. We had 27 percent of the market. We were leading the pack, so you could say Chevrolet wasn't doing

In 1925, Felix Chevrolet sold a new business coupe. Decades later, Nick Shammas heard one of the cars was available and couldn't resist acquiring the artifact for the Felix showroom.

too many bad things. Ed Cole was making many of the decisions, and he was quite a guy—a genius."

Small, rural dealerships were still alive and well in the late 1950s, making their livings and allocations along the dusty dirt roads and two-lane highways of the West by selling trucks to farmers and still taking prewar cars in on trade. While these gritty tales hold fascination for classic-era car buffs, Felix Chevrolet reached for the glamour and glitter of show business for its promotion. The dealership dressed for success, and handsome, dapper Nick Shammas posed and spoke for the cameras like the movie stars at the Shrine Auditorium.

"I was on television in those days. I used to go to the fights, and people would want my autograph. I finally got tired of it, and I said, 'Listen, I *pay* to be on TV. When I *get paid* to be on, then you can get my autograph.' We did three-minute commercials in those days, and I would line all my people up and introduce them. We were all over the dial, seven days a week, on KTLA in particular. Originally, the commercials were live, but thank God, we got tape later on.

"I had a lot of crazy experiences doing commercials. I had gone up to Channel 13 [KCOP] and had done my commercial, but they were showing an old movie, and the film kept breaking. I was finished, but [the director signaled me] and I had to ad-lib for another minute or two—live!—and if you don't know what that's like, I'm here to tell you, it's pretty rough.

"I got into a little trouble when I had the world champion boxer Joe Louis on. Joe Louis talked very slow, and when you're doing a commercial, you've got to get through it. I had introduced him by saying, 'I'm here with Joe Louis, one of the great world champions of boxing,' and the mail *poured in,* saying, 'What about Jack Dempsey?!' Joe Louis did all right on the commercial. He had his boxing matches in Las Vegas, and here we had Earl Carroll's on Sunset Boulevard where they had boxing every Friday night. I had Joe Louis on every week to talk about boxing."

In 1925, Felix Chevrolet had sold a new business coupe. Around 1960, Nick Shammas heard the car was available and couldn't resist having the artifact for the Felix showroom.

"The man who bought the car new had died, and his wife still had the car. We bought the car. We also bought her a coat with fur on it, and we bought her a beautiful wristwatch and some other things. We brought the car here. It was my pride and joy, and we had it here on the showroom floor. This happened about 1965. A fellow who was drunk plowed through this signal at Figueroa and Jefferson and went through my showroom floor. I wouldn't have cared if he had hit all the new cars, but of all the cars, he went right into that special one. It was in immaculate condition with the Felix license frames, and it had the Felix step plates on the running boards. I fixed it up."

Branching out seems to have been Shammas' theme from the very first little lot he had in Hollywood, and this instinctive urge to expand into larger areas caused Shammas to take on additional franchises that took Felix Chevrolet safely through the gas crunch in the

He may have lost his head to time and weather, but Felix the Cat still greets passengers from the dash of this 1933 Chevrolet. The car resides in the Tom Meleo collection. It was bought new at Felix Chevrolet.

No doubt a competitor of Felix Chevrolet, Relph Chevrolet of Los Angeles placed his moniker on the dash of this 1937 Chevrolet in the Tom Meleo collection.

1970s and other economic forces in the 1980s and 1990s.

"In '59, I opened a Volkswagen store. That was the first branching out to other makes we did. After Volkswagen came Porsche, and we eventually took on Mitsubishi. We also brought in Subaru, and I wish I had kept it because we were the distributor for Subaru, but at that time, you had to mix the oil and gas. Later on, Subaru eliminated the need to mix oil and gas, and they were all right, but by then, someone else already had the distributorship, and it was too late for me to get it back. No one who knew anything about the car business would have taken on Subaru when you still had to mix fuel, but it turned out to be good in the end, so sometimes ignorance is helpful. Shortly after we opened George Chevrolet in Bellflower in about 1969, we took on Mercedes, and that was the most spectacular thing we ever did. By 1980, we had become the largest Mercedes-Benz dealer in the country, bar none."

Around Shammas' luxurious office are the artifacts of other times: a Quality Dealer Award from Chevrolet of late-1950s vintage, photos of his much admired predecessor Bill Felix, and a beautiful ashtray from Chevrolet sales hero William Holler, inscribed to "my good friend Bill Felix." For nearly 50 years, Shammas has proudly worked at Bill Felix's large, sturdy, tastefully ornate desk. The respect and admiration for Bill Felix can be heard in Shammas' voice at every mention of Felix's name. Bill Felix's shoes were big shoes to fill, especially for a young man not yet 40 years old. But Shammas excelled, and the Felix and Shammas names will be linked in Chevrolet and Los Angeles lore for as long as there are cars on the humming Harbor Freeway.

"I worked very hard. I was frightened when I first stepped into Felix Chevrolet. I had never been in a business that big. I had worked very hard during the war, and knowing the toll that kind of hard work can take, I told my wife I would only keep Felix Chevrolet for a couple of years. That was 1955, and I'm still at it."

O'Rielly Chevrolet

Frank C. O'Rielly learned the automobile business by working in a Cadillac dealership in Tucson, Arizona. He opened his own Chevrolet franchise in March 1924 and built this location in 1929. To secure financing for the construction, O'Rielly had to assure the lenders that the building would suit more than one purpose. Therefore, the building was designed from the start to be quickly converted into a bowling alley if the car business didn't work out. The tall structure on the roof was a high-volume evaporative cooler. It made it possible for Chevrolet customers—or bowlers—to go about their business in comfort, protected from the hot Arizona sun. O'Rielly operated at this location until 1964. *O'Rielly Motor Company collection*

A 1961 O'Rielly Motor Company billboard. Although none of this would interest the horse in the photograph, the billboard on a highway near Tucson harkens back to Frank O'Rielly's earliest days in the car business. "A lot of the time, when my father sold a car in the 1920s, he had to teach people how to drive it," Buck O'Rielly tells. "It's only a couple of hours from Tucson to Phoenix now, but in the early days, it used to be about a 10- or 12-hour trip, and you had to figure you were going to change at least one tire along the way. In the rainy season, you had to take a shovel along because you were going to have to dig yourself out of a[n] arroyo. You could really go to Phoenix easier on a train than you could with a car. He used to sell to ranchers and the Indian tribes. He'd go on the reservations, take his typewriter, and type out the contract on the hood of the car. They had a car come back to the service department, and this Indian had bought a four-door sedan, taken the rear seat out, and he had a couple of calves in there. He was using it to haul cattle. You never knew what people were going to use their cars for." *O'Rielly Motor Company collection*

When a circus came to Tucson, Frank O'Rielly got the "giant" to pose for some promotional photographs to prove a Chevrolet could be comfortable for anyone. O'Rielly family lore has it that this man was about 7 feet, 5 inches. He's seen here stepping into a rumble seat in a single bound. *O'Rielly Motor Company collection*

An official Chevrolet dealership ink blotter features the model 490 monogrammed especially for the O'Rielly Motor Company as a showroom giveaway. *O'Rielly Motor Company collection*

$490
f. o. b. Flint, Mich.

for Economical Transportation

CHEVROLET

SUPERIOR
2-Passenger **ROADSTER**

YOUR dollar buys the most transportation with this Chevrolet---price, operation and maintenance considered. In addition you get up-to-the-minute style, handsome finish, and full modern equipment.

Five-Passenger Touring	$495
Two-Passenger Utility Coupe	640
Five-Passenger Sedan	795

f. o. b. Flint, Mich.

O'RIELLY MOTOR CO., Inc.
51 to 57 North Sixth Avenue   TUCSON, ARIZONA

NOTHING COMPARES WITH CHEVROLET

HOLZ MOTORS—HALES CORNER, WISCONSIN

On the Road to Janesville

"You can shear a sheep once a year, but you can skin him only once," says Jerry Holz of Holz Motors, the number-one car dealership in the state of Wisconsin. As late as 1960, Holz Motors only had room for three cars in its showroom, fronting 108th Street in Hales Corners, a small farming community that suburban Milwaukee is creeping toward and slowly enveloping. Holz's statement of honesty may have played a role in growing the once humble dealership into a leading enterprise.

By the time Jerry Holz was born in 1927, his father, R. W. Holz, had been in the Chevrolet business for 12 years, having left a secure job with a railroad in hopes of trading his coal shovel for the exciting new frontier of the automobile industry. In those heady days, American car companies were coming, going, merging, and eating each other at a frenetic rate. R. W. Holz's first two automotive products, the K.R.I.T. and then the Imperial, were both out of business within six months of Holz taking them on. Today, Chevrolet is a household name throughout most of the world and has spent many seasons in America's number-one spot. But in 1915, Chevrolet was no safer a bet for Holz than K.R.I.T. or Imperial had been. Holz bet everything on the automobile at a time when gasoline was delivered to the dealership's service station with a horse and wagon.

R. W. and Gertrude Holz lived with their growing family in a small apartment above their dealership. Jerry was the youngest of five children and speaks with open admiration of his father's earliest efforts.

"At that time, Ford was the dominant thing, and no one had heard of Chevrolets," Jerry tells. "It took guts to go up against that. At that time, a lot of cars were put up for the winter, and no one was driving in the winter. We had what we called the rapid transit—an electric railway running all over Milwaukee and out to some of the farther-flung suburbs and towns. It went quite a few miles. He would take an order book with

Holz Motors of Hales Corners, Wisconsin—the Badger State's largest-selling car dealership of any brand.

some pamphlets and brochures, and he would go as far as the electric railroad would go and walk to wherever he could find customers. The farmers weren't busy in the winter either. He would walk to the farms and take orders. He was basically a door-to-door salesman—certainly different from the way we sell cars today."

Jerry Holz's earliest memories of his father's practices begin in the 1930s with his child's-eye view of the Great Depression's symptoms and his father's reactions to Chevrolet's sales department leader, William Holler.

"We were poor as dirt, but we never knew it because everybody else was in the same boat. We always had enough to eat, clean clothes,

and a roof over our head, so what more do you need? At that time, my father would come back from any sales meeting [William Holler] would have, and someone was *going to buy* a car. Bill Holler had a knack for getting people enthused to sell. He was instrumental in putting Chevrolet on the map as the number-one dealer for years. It was the Quality Dealer Program, and it's too bad we got away from it. Take care of the customer, what a concept! It was one of the best things to ever happen to Chevrolet, and they should bring it back—lock, stock, and barrel—just as it was. I recall one sentence Holler was talking about everything Chevrolet, and his last sentence was, 'Sell like hell!' That was his

message. When Dad came back from a meeting, I'm telling you, he was excited. If you're wondering what put Chevrolet in first place, it was William Holler."

The Depression eased, but World War II loomed. Some dealerships stockpiled cars, parts, and supplies well in advance, while others sold off entire inventories—some feared being driven out of business and wanted the cash to get through the war, and some simply wanted to take the duration off as a vacation. R. W. Holz was somewhere in between, not gathering tons of extra parts, but still making preparations to stick with the car business and survive on the service department.

The Industrial Revolution brought new and mighty words into common language: dynamo, turbine, high-voltage. At one time, "battery" meant a series of cannons, but in the 1890s, it came to mean a series of electric cells powering a new mechanized world. The Milwaukee Electric Railway and Light Company began laying its tracks in 1897, and by the early twentieth century, Milwaukee became one of several big American cities with a modern, efficient, high-speed public transportation system. Many of the lines reached well beyond Milwaukee's city limits and took tourists through rolling countryside to southeast Wisconsin's "lake country" resorts.

In 1915, a young man boarded the electric rail line in Hales Corners, a small farming town southwest of Milwaukee. He was holding brochures in one hand and a sales order book in the other. He was getting on an efficient, easy-to-use electric railroad to convince people to buy automobiles at a time when cars cost as much as houses, gasoline was sold in gallon jugs in drug stores, and roads were just muddy ruts. R. W. Holz staked his living on the future, putting gleaming highways right next to America's railroad tracks.

By the 1930s, Milwaukee's electric rails were in sharp decline. The personal freedom of the automobile had taken over, but through several ownerships, name changes, and abandonments of its lines, the electric rails still limped along after World War II.

Jay E. Maeder of Cleveland, Ohio, was a railroad devotee and hobbyist. In 1949, he bought Milwaukee's only two remaining interurban lines for a whopping $110 and changed the company name to Speedrail. Maeder was determined to make Milwaukee's electric rails succeed again.

September 2, 1950, began as a happy day for Speedrail. Maeder was hosting charter trips for the National Model Railroad Association on the Waukesha and Hales Corners lines. On his first run to Hales Corners, Maeder proudly took the controls of the trolley with an experienced motorman standing by as the law required. Maeder and the happy group of railroad hobbyists were riding one of the old lightweight streetcars. Up ahead, one of Milwaukee's heavyweights was coming around a curve and barreling down a hill at full cruising speed. The two met head-on. The lightweight trolley didn't stand a chance, and ten lives ended in a split second. Maeder jumped from the trolley just in time and survived. A series of investigations acquitted him of blame, but he was a ruined man.

The crash ended electric railways in Milwaukee and secured the automobile's supremacy as principle transportation. But today, Jerry Holz, heir to the most successful car dealership of any brand in the state of Wisconsin, points sadly to the easement through the woods where the tracks once were. The electric rail tracks took his father on his first sales calls in the automobile business.

which worked out because there were no cars to sell anyway."

Jerry Holz joined the Army Air Corps upon graduating from high school in 1944. While in an accelerated education program in Michigan, Holz was stricken with a near-fatal pneumonia. With the war over, Holz served with the occupying forces in Germany. What he came home to was the beginning of the sunny, optimistic growth of postwar America's jet age. Rocket-shaped car bodies dripped with chrome and were priced so that even blue-collar guys could afford them. Before the war, a teenaged Holz had worked in the dealership pumping gas and checking oil; after the war, he returned to the dealership and began his own 60-year destiny with Chevrolet.

"I started absolutely at the bottom, and I have great respect for people who work with their hands. I don't look down at anybody. I respect them as human beings. I started out in the service department greasing cars and changing oil."

Holz saw a lot of broken axles and springs. They were fairly common Chevrolet ailments in the 1940s, and in Wisconsin, mufflers only lasted about a year.

"If you got 12,000 miles out of a set of tires, you were going great. You learned how to use hot patches, cold patches, and how to make these tires last. To grind the valves on an overhead-valve Chevrolet was a common practice, as were pistons and pins. There were no insert bearings in those Chevrolet engines—Janesville vibrators, as we called them. They had babbitt bearings right in the rods, and you had a sturdy vice and a bastard file. If you could turn the rod on the crank, you had it right enough, and if not, you had to shim the bearing caps out one or two thousandths. Those were good lessons to be learned by all technicians. We had people who were great at grinding valves, fixing standard transmissions, clutches, and other things."

The postwar boom was on, but Hales Corners was still a farming community. Late in the 1947 season, General Motors introduced a new truck line featuring curvy good looks, far better driver comfort, and in the following seasons,

"We called it pickling the cars," Holz recalls. "We would put them up on blocks to keep them up off the tires. We would pull the spark plugs and spray some kind of preservative into the cylinders. Everything was rationed—gasoline, tires, everything. The business survived by service work. Our cars came shipped with water in them those years. One of the big projects was to put antifreeze in all the cars. It was a big project to winterize cars for people. It was a yearly thing to replace hoses and fan belts [and those things still needed to be done for people during the war]. A lot of the guys who worked in dealerships at the time were in the military,

In 1917, the corner of 108th Street and Janesville Road in Hales Corners, Wisconsin, was home to two-year-old Holz Motors. R. W. Holz would ride the electric train into Milwaukee and beyond to sell cars door to door. When Holz Motors first opened its service station, gasoline was delivered to the station by horse and wagon. Holz and his young family lived in the apartment above the dealership's service bay. *Holz Motors collection*

five-window cabs with available trim packages. GM called the line Advance Design.

"We had a lot of truck farmers around here with vegetable crops," Holz recalls. "We sold a lot of ton-and-a-half trucks, with eight-and-a-quarter tires on them. There were a lot of good things about the Advance Design trucks. In those days, trucks were trucks. They were tools and [the best we'd ever had up to that point]."

Philosophically, Hales Corners seemed worlds away from nearby Milwaukee, and the Holz showroom still only held three cars. Jerry Holz took his turn and began reliving some of his father's previous experiences as he eased toward the dealership's helm.

"Again, we were dirt poor, but we didn't know it," Holz says with a nostalgic smile and a knowing look. "I was married three days before my twenty-first birthday. Dorothy and I have been married well over 50 years, and we lived in that apartment above the service garage, and that it was called a *garage* at that time explains how we made our living. If your sales volume wasn't huge, you did a lot of service work. My gosh, today, we're up to $71 an hour for labor, but I think we started out at something like one dollar an hour, flat rate, for labor. We had an old cash register—a big, clunky thing—that only went up to $9,999, and it's hard to think that we were selling cars for under four figures. The keys [for the high thousands] were brand new because we never had any occasion to use them."

Holz says he would be up to his elbows working on a car in the service garage, and when a sale beckoned, he would wipe the grease off his hands and become a salesman.

"[Even after the war], the cars still didn't even have antifreeze in them when they arrived. That was a big project every fall. I'd hate to even

The New KRIT

KRIT (K.R.I.T.) (US) 1909-1916
Krit Motor Co., Detroit, Mich.
Early models of the Krit were small three- and four-seaters with 4-cylinder engines. For 1911, a two-seater with an underslung chassis was built. The last models of this make were classed as light cars, with a 3.6-litre 4-cylinder engine. The price was $850 for either the roadster or touring version.

A Sensation Among 1914 Motor Cars

At the New York Show the new Krit Special Touring Car — with five demountable wire wheels, handsome seat covers, one-man top and a host of other features — was adjudged a 1914 sensation among motor cars. At local shows in many parts of the country this verdict is receiving an endorsement in terms of orders for the new Krit.

"Two years ahead of the field" is one comment and it strikes the keynote.

It has been felt that a car at the price of the Krit would come — a car with quality features of cars at three and four times the price. Manufacturers have been working toward this end. Motorists have been watching with expectation.

And now here comes the 1914 Krit to meet the demands of those motorists who demand the best and latest in style, comfort and convenience, together with mechanical excellence and economical operating cost.

Compare the new Krit point by point, with the highest priced cars. You will find it lacking in no features you may desire in a motor car: streamline body, tapered bonnet, rounded radiator, graceful fenders, handsome electric lights, left drive, clear-vision, double ventilating windshield, carburetor adjustment from steering column, gasoline tank in dash, tire carrier at rear and so on.

Small wonder then that one dealer has wired an order for 50 new Krits, that another wants his allotment increased, and that others are equally enthusiastic.

Write and secure our dealer's proposition in your own territory. The new Krit carries an immediate appeal. It is the car that motorists have been waiting for.

Best of All at the Price

This new Krit Special Touring Car sells at $1,050; with electric starter, $1,150.

KRIT MOTOR CAR COMPANY
Detroit, Mich.

R. W. Holz decided to leave the security of the railroad business and venture into the exciting new world of automobiles in 1915. His first product was K.R.I.T., a high-quality, four-cylinder car built in Detroit from 1910 to 1915. One six-cylinder model was produced for 1913. *Holz Motors collection*

think about doing it today, but whatever inventory we had, we had to drain the water out of them and put in the antifreeze ourselves. I myself installed rearview mirrors, clocks, windshield washers, directional signals, seat covers, overflow tanks, fancy wheel covers, and underseat heaters. Today, if they wanted to have a nice feature in an automobile, it would be the underseat heaters because that was a great idea. There was a manufacturer by the name of Fulton right here in West Allis, and they made those sun shades that came in a green primer, and you had to paint them to match the car. They were adjustable and made to fit any car. [When it came time to be a salesman], I had a favorite route. I would take them down Double-O, which was a rough road. I'd take the car off the pavement onto the shoulder to show them how well it handled. There was a cut-out where I'd get out of the car and invite the prospect to drive the car. There was a new road right here behind the dealership where they could feel how smooth the car drove on a good road."

As luxury items filtered down to the low-priced field, Chevrolet's offering for those who wanted more convenient driving was Powerglide. GM's nonshifting, torque converter–based transmission was fitted onto Chevrolets as the marque's first automatic.

"Times weren't that different from now," Holz says. "People don't change that rapidly, especially in that older generation. Today, people expect new products more [often]. Powerglide wasn't the fastest transmission offered in the market, but it was dependable, and once you got used to it, it was smooth and nice to drive. You drove differently then, also. The roads were different, and you anticipated."

The *Happy Days* television version of the 1950s is not altogether accurate, but there were certain events the public enjoyed at the time that even those purists now look back on pleasantly and wish to relive. Every fall, the curtains were hung in dealership windows, cars were hidden in service departments, searchlights were rented, VIPs were allowed sneak peeks, and when announcement day finally rolled around, people took the kids and made a party of seeing the new models.

"The old dealership building had a lower level in it—a basement," Holz remembers. "It was a perfect place to put the new cars before the announcement, and we would have a pre-announcement party the night before. Every dealer had a representative model of the new products. You didn't have a lot of them, but you had demonstrators, and you would take orders from customers. It was an exciting time, and people looked forward to it. We used to throw a pretty good lunch and have a keg of beer around. It was a great excuse to throw a party. Nineteen fifty-five was a complete change in style, and the biggest news was the V-8 engine. It was well timed and really well accepted. It won a lot of races, but I think they made a lot of improvements on that early V-8 engine in a short amount of time. I don't think the early ones were that well made, but they stepped up to the plate, and today it's still a standard GM engine. I would say that announcement was a bit more exciting than average, but we still only had room for three cars in our showroom."

It's hard for Holz to pin down a particular model or year as his favorite.

"They were all favorites at that time. Nineteen fifty-nine was a very controversial model. The nice thing about the 1959 and '60s models was that the customers either liked them or hated them. That was even more true for the '57 than the '59. The '57 didn't have the public appeal. Ford had a new model. It's amazing today that the '57s are one of the hottest cars from the collector's standpoint. At that time, Chevrolet was riding the crest of the 1955 models along with the nice '56s. It wasn't even close for second place, but then, we got the '57s, Ford caught up to us with a brand-new product that was more accepted than our Chevrolets. It just shows that people buy from appearances.

"Thinking about [GM President] Bob Lutz, he finally owned General Motors up to the fact that it's the product that sells. You can call it whatever you want, but when it comes down to it, people don't necessarily buy new cars because they need them. They want something new and exciting, and as long as we keep offering that, we'll have a successful business. Back in

Holz had only been a K.R.I.T. dealer for a few months when the company went bankrupt. Undaunted, Holz took on Imperial, one of several companies to use the regal name before it was relegated to the Chryslers of the 1920s. Like K.R.I.T., Imperial suffered a quick demise when its founding pair of brothers left their Jackson, Michigan, plant to go to work for Hupp. Once again, Holz was a dealer without a franchise, and when he took on the four-year-old Chevrolet company's products, it was no safer a bet than K.R.I.T. or Imperial had been. *Holz Motors collection*

Holz Motors in the 1940s. R. W. Holz's youngest son, Jerry, was born in 1927. When Jerry began his career with his father's dealership, he and his wife, Dorothy, lived in the apartment above the service department, just as his parents had. *Holz Motors collection*

the era of the announcement days, General Motors changed the cars from year to year. You could see a car from the front, back, or side and know what year it was. People would see them, and they would want that new car, and we had the ability to trade automobiles. I think the lowest in those days for trading one year's difference was about $200, with many of the trade-ins getting up to about $500. There were advantages to the new-car buyer that helped him get into the new car he wanted. Today, it's all a matter of dollars. If you establish that a car depreciates 25 percent a year, what's 25 percent of $30,000?

"[The year] '58 put us back in first place. They were much more attractive. They had the [optional] air-ride suspension. You'd go out there in the morning, and it was sitting funny, and you'd have to wait for the air compressor to fill up the bags again. We replaced a lot of those systems and put the springs back in."

If the 1959 Chevrolet was a controversial design, the 1958 window-sticker law was a controversial bill. Unlike Bud Webster in Cody, Wyoming, Jerry Holz believed the root problem needed to be resolved.

"[The window-sticker law] addressed the reasons that many dealers had a bad reputation

they probably earned," Holz explains. "You have to put that into perspective that this was a smaller town at that time, and I don't think we had the desire to sell over sticker. If you take a 2003 anniversary Corvette, there are probably dealers who would sell that for way over sticker, but we look at the MSRP, and that's what we sell any car for. That's probably the reason the sticker wound up there in the first place."

Holz maintains that, unlike in smaller towns where a dealer's behavior was kept in check by the quick spread of any hint of wrongdoing, dealers in more urban areas were getting away with practices that threatened the whole

Hales Corners finally caught up to the modern, postwar world, and in 1962, Holz Motors built a new facility a half-block to the south of the building where it all began. The original Holz Motors building is just out of frame to the right. *Holz Motors collection*

industry. The factory's ability to raise prices was something he just had to learn to accept.

"One of the things I try to keep learning in the automobile business is that I have little or no control over what the factory does," Holz adds. "I have to be able to deal with the hand I get dealt. It's an ongoing balancing act. It's a miracle we've been able to survive some of the management policies [during certain periods]. It's an amazing thing. There's only one reason in the world dealers are successful: They're not smarter than anybody else and maybe dumber than some, but they have the ability to trade. If that weren't true, Wal-Mart could sell automobiles because they could put them in there at whatever price they wanted, and the customer could take it to the cashier and drive it away, but what would they do with the trade-ins? Car dealers perform a function that nobody else has found a way to do better."

Controversy brewed again with the introduction of Chevrolet's rear-engine, air-cooled Corvair in 1960.

"Corvair was a brand-new product. In the late '50s, the cars were getting so big, you couldn't get them into the garage. Chevrolet's answer to the feeling [for the need] for a smaller car was the Corvair. It was a radical change. It had an air-cooled rear engine and a lot of other good features. [But] the engine leaked like a sieve because they were all aluminum, and they weren't as sophisticated as the aluminum castings are today. We had a technician who's long retired, and he made a living on Corvairs keeping them running and fixing the oil leaks. They had their place. They were pretty good in the snow because the engine had its weight on the drive wheels. The only trouble was, if the snow was too deep, it would act like a sled and get up on top of the snow and slide around. If it wasn't too deep, they were great. Of course, if the snow's that deep, you probably shouldn't have been driving anyway. Taking the customers out in the snow in the Corvairs was the fun part of demonstrating them. The Corvairs weren't as bad as [Ralph] Nader said."

Corvair sold nearly 250,000 units in its first year, dispelling the myth that it was a poor seller.

describes the dealership's growth to number one in Wisconsin as steady, with a few spikes along the way.

"It's like the car business—steady growth, but some years are better than others. The biggest spike was 1988. We had just put a further addition on the building, and it gave us a new appearance in keeping with the growing economics of the time. The whole area has just been growing, and we're hopefully keeping ahead of it."

At the dawning of the twenty-first century, Holz Motors is in the Badger State's number-one spot. It has 35 salespeople and boasts a record of supporting community efforts, such as the Milwaukee County Zoo. The dealership operates in the tradition of the Quality Dealer Program with a humble man at the helm.

"I never forgot where I came from. I don't consider myself a wealthy man. Success is a four-letter word spelled W-O-R-K. Anybody who uses that word will be as successful as he can possibly be," says Holz. "People sometimes look at this dealership and say, 'My God, how do you sell all those cars?' I tell them, 'One at a time.'"

Holz Motors sparkling under a summer moon in the 1960s. *Holz Motors collection*

Huge sales of Ford's Falcon and respectable sales of Chrysler's technologically advanced Valiants and Lancers made General Motors want to offer a more conventional, less experimental small car in the low-priced field. Chevrolet's answer was the good-looking, quickly conceived Chevy II.

"I think GM's perspective on the Chevy II at the time was, 'Well, we've got to build this damned small car, so let's build one and get it over with,'" Holz remembers. "I think GM forgot they were selling them to customers. Chevy II served a purpose at the time, and it was a radical design from the standpoint that it didn't have a frame—a unibody. It was OK, but it didn't have the public appeal. It was kind of a joke for a while, and even when they finally put the V-8 in them, there was one spark plug down by the frame that was really hard to get at."

Holz reports that Camaros were great sellers for his dealership, but the public's taste for speed was curtailed by the OPEC oil embargo in 1973 and 1974 and the resulting gas lines.

"It affected the lease company the most, because the big gas guzzlers, as we called them at the time, were practically sale-proof. We took a big hit on them when the leases terminated, and the big cars came back as used cars. You could usually figure a pretty good residual if people took care of them, but the big cars were just sale-proof under those conditions."

In the 1960s, the Holz family enterprise was still very much as it had been in 1915. Holz

The Holz Motors mission statement above the glowing neon points the way to Jerry's Pro Shop, Holz Motors' retail shop of Chevrolet accessories and NASCAR merchandise.

Pinky Randall

One of the finest private assemblages of Chevrolet dealership memorabilia resides in the capable hands of noted Chevrolet historian and collector Pinky Randall of Michigan. The help he offers historians, writers, and Chevrolet enthusiasts is well known and beyond calculation.
Pinky Randall collection

SMITH CHEVROLET—ATLANTA, GEORGIA

One Hundred Twenty-five Years and Five Points
The daily grind of making a living doesn't usually invoke images of dukes, earls, counts, or barons, but this is America, where hard work, perseverance, and family loyalty have built common people's dynasties.

A boy was born in Ireland in 1835. The Emerald Isle's potato famine drove the boy, christened John Morton Smith, to Canada.

At the age of 14, he moved to the United States. He was good with his hands and learned the all-important carriage-building trade. He surrounded himself with wooden wheels, suspension springs, steering mechanisms, parking brakes, and axle grease. When John Morton Smith went into business for himself in 1869, he could not have known that these carriage-trade terms and skills would cement his name onto a family business that would last into the 1990s.

In 1876, John Morton Smith had a son, John Edward Smith, who was known as Captain John. The family line entered the twentieth century with the birth of Hal Smith in 1904 and John Smith III in 1935. Hal and John III remember the good days and bad days of dealing Chevrolets in Atlanta, Georgia, and tell the stories in a low, patient Southern accent. They speak with distinct admiration of the first of their family to live in America.

The family's carriage company started in 1869 as McBride and Smith on Atlanta's Broad Street but soon became simply the John Smith Company. Historian Franklin Garrett's book *Atlanta and Its Environs* reports, "Within a few years, everyone came to know that a Smith carriage was one with every bolt of steel and every spoke of hickory."

Captain John was only a year old in 1877 when the Georgia State Agriculture Society had bestowed its Best Family Carriage award on the John Smith Company.

"About 1881, my great-grandfather built a factory at 120, 122, and 124 Wheat Street, which was later changed to the famous Auburn Street where Martin Luther King's church was," John Smith III tells. "That building was finally demolished in the early 1970s, although we hadn't owned it in a long time by then. Atlanta Life Insurance has that property now. We operated in that location until my grandfather, Captain John, built a building at 530 West Peachtree Street, and we were there until December of 1976 when we moved to 2155 Cobb Parkway. The post office for the Cobb Parkway location is Smyrna, Georgia, but it was out in the country on Highway 41. It was fairly rural at that time. Highway 41 was the main road between Atlanta and the Bell Aircraft plant where the B-29 was built. Highway 41 was the first four-lane highway in Georgia, and it was built for the war effort."

The act of building carriages was taken seriously and was viewed as a science. Thus, Captain John sought the science's education.

"Captain John graduated from Georgia Tech, and he went to New York City to study carriage design," John III continues. "He

"My grandfather had a policy that we would trade for anything. We still have a cemetery plot somewhere from a trade," John Smith tells. At Smith Chevrolet's West Peachtree Street location around 1930, (L–R) an unknown man tends the donkey. Alongside him stand Shang Reed, "Captain John" Smith, Barney Stodghill, and a Mr. Shacklefoot, known as Mr. Shack. Reed and Shack were sales managers at the time. *John Smith III collection*

For untold thousands of years, it went unseen by human eyes—a granite rib in the wilderness, strangled by jungle. Later, people called Cherokee walked over it. The French crossed it, and finally, English was heard on it. There was no reason for a town to be anywhere near the ridge until coal burned in cast iron, steam breathed through cylinders, and heavy steel wheels rolled down twin tracks. Marietta and Decatur were full-fledged towns when the steel rails finally connected them to Chattanooga. The granite ridge intersected with other ridge lines and forced the railroad tracks to intersect there, too, and in the middle of nowhere, the Western and Atlantic Railroad's mile marker number zero branded the spot. This intersection between the towns became important to each community and finally became a town itself, first called Terminus. Later it was renamed Marthasville, after the governor's daughter.

Marietta Street and Decatur Street head northwest and east to their respective towns from Zero Mile Marker, and Edgewood Avenue and Whitehall Street meet there, too. The once lonely granite rib was affectionately named Peachtree Ridge, and the street atop it held some of the city's finest homes. When rain falls on the west side of Peachtree Street, gravity takes it to the Flint River, where it eventually finds the Gulf of Mexico. When rain falls on the east side of Peachtree Street, it splashes into the Savannah River and disappears eastward into the city's namesake. Marthasville was too long a name for the railroad schedules, and the city took on a feminized version of the great ocean where the Savannah River disappears.

Atlanta, Georgia, assumed its name in 1845, and it became official two years later. When the natives talk about the center of the city, they're talking about Five Points, where the railroad's Zero Mile Marker brought the five wagon roads together. This intersection was essential for the South to protect and essential for the North to destroy. The burning of Atlanta was a tragedy for both sides—a gross but necessary war-ending maneuver.

Five Points bustled into the Guilded Age as a meeting place for business, politics, and society. It was where Coca-Cola was created in 1887 by Dr. Pemberton, a Five Points local. In 1869, a young Irishman named Smith began building high-quality wagons and carriages in Five Points. As the decades passed, he never completely accepted that the ancient, permanent-seeming carriage-building arts would go out of style. But with blinding suddenness, the automobile did indeed take over. Smith's descendants embraced the automobile, and the family name would be connected to Atlanta's automobile trade for nearly 100 years to follow.

There was a downside to automobiles, as summed up by the proprietor of a former Five Points institution. Thomas Pitts' cigar store and soda fountain was a friendly meeting place for Atlanta socializing, and the phrase "Meet me at Pitts" was how many social gatherings were initiated. In his book Atlanta and Its Environs, prominent Atlanta historian Franklin Garrett quoted Thomas Pitts lamenting that Five Points had "become a thoroughfare instead of a center. . . . Hundreds used to stop; now thousands pass. . . . Now, instead of having one community center, Atlanta has many. In the old days, people used to go 'to town' in the evening, Now, they take their cars and ride away from town, and at night, Five Points is almost deserted. People used to stroll down on Sunday morning to buy the paper and a cigar, and perhaps get a drink before going to church, but they don't do that anymore."

Mr. Pitts closed his famous store in 1926.

The automobile may have destroyed some of the area's sense of community, but on the flip side, it brought prosperity to Atlanta and self-determined transportation to its citizens. In the 1930s, William Holler was the dynamic force behind Chevrolet sales at the corporate level, and very often he would hold up Coca-Cola as the world's best franchise. Smith Chevrolet once hosted a meeting at its Five Points location for all the Chevrolet dealers in the Atlanta area where Holler gave his usual enthusiastic performance and forceful advice. As he held up his examples, did Holler know he was standing in the place where the "world's best franchise" had been invented?

away. My grandfather said, 'As long as you're looking for a new Buick dealer in Decatur, you might as well look for a new one in Atlanta.' In 1924, my grandfather took on Chevrolet. Our first ad for Chevrolet was in early August of 1924."

Hal Smith reached adulthood in the 1920s and became generation number three in the Smith enterprise.

"My father took on the Chevrolet dealership in 1924," Hal Smith recalls. "I was a young man about 20 years old. I remember going out to the Chevrolet regional office in Atlanta and seeing my father sign the contract. I got invited along because I wanted to see it. Chevrolet had kind of a warehouse with cars and parts everywhere, and that's where the regional office was."

Chevrolet had hit pay dirt in 1916 with the introduction of its famous Model 490, named for its base selling price. The 490 was outmoded by 1923, and Chevrolet's base four-cylinder car was the Superior. It was much more smoothly designed and mechanically modern than its predecessor, but it was still very much a 1920s economy car when the Smiths took it on in 1924.

"We took that baby on, and it had what was called the cone clutch," Hal recalls. "It had the reputation for holding the record for the broad jump! It was almost impossible to let the clutch out easily so the car wouldn't jump. They came out with the disc clutch in 1925, but before that, the cone clutch would jump [a] country mile when you let it out! I remember working in the shop and replacing all those rear ends because the cone clutch had jerked them loose. The disc clutch made it possible to move that car into a sales position to where it would sell. The six-cylinder engine [in 1929] was a good thing. They came out with the overhead valves, and it was a remarkably good motor and a remarkable car, but really, it was the disc clutch that saved the day."

The Great Depression crashed down on the United States and the world in October 1929. Eventually, bread lines and violent strikes hit the industrialized cities, and starving refugees fled the Midwest's Dust Bowl. Hal

came back in 1898 and went to work with his father. My great-grandfather John M. Smith died in 1913 and never did believe in automobiles. My grandfather started selling cars in 1906. He sold REOs, Pierce Arrows, Chalmers, Saxons, Apperson Jack Rabbits, Hudsons. In 1913, he took on Buick, at the same time he had REO. There was some kind of disagreement between my grandfather and Buick. The Buick manager came to my grandfather and asked him to help find a dealer in Decatur, which is about six miles

Presidents Club
Opening of CHEVROLET PLANT
May 1928

The members of Chevrolet's President's Club attend the opening of a new Chevrolet plant on Sawtell Road in Atlanta in May 1928. "Captain John" Smith can be seen toward the right of the photo standing with his hat in his left hand. "In the early days, my grandfather kept a deposit with Chevrolet," John Smith III explains. "When [cars allotted to him] were manufactured, he would send someone out there to get the cars, and General Motors would essentially debit his account. When the account got low, they would call up Mr. Stodghill, and he would send someone with a check out to Sawtell Road. My grandfather paid for his cars directly—a long time ago, before the electronics got so fancy. *John Smith III collection*

Smith was in his prime when he had to face the toughest of times.

"Atlanta didn't escape the Depression," Hal recalls. "People in businesses of all types suffered from it. We were not in the country where people bartered cows and things like that. I think we might have bartered some for oil and parts, but I don't recall it being a major part of our business."

William Holler, the luminary driving force of the Chevrolet sales organization through the darkest hours of the Great Depression, made his usual impression on Hal Smith. Like almost all Chevrolet dealers of the time, Smith recalls Holler being an energetic motivator who took the Great Depression's fears and turned them into a force to succeed. Holler's efforts and his Quality Dealer Program cemented Chevrolet customer loyalty for decades to come.

Bill Holler was one of the greatest salespeople General Motors ever had," recalls Hal Smith. "He really put a lot of spunk and get-up-and-go into Chevrolet. He was a remarkable man. The quality of the automobiles improved at that time, and Bill Holler put Chevrolet on the map. He would have dealer meetings right out on the sales floor for all the dealers in our area, and he could really fire you up, I tell you that, right out. He knew how to put the together items that would interest a sales organization. The dealers were interested in what kind of discount they got in relation to the retail market. They were interested in making money, and they were interested in the salesmen making money. This is where Holler was so good. He'd get the salesmen fired up, and they would do a good job. There's no doubt about that.

"[The Quality Dealer Program] was one of his great ideas. It appealed to the salesmen because quality was important then. He had a great capacity to excite and inspire men to do better and get ahead of the game. I remember the program requiring that the cars had been thoroughly inspected before they were delivered to the customers. It had to do with that kind of salesmen the dealerships had and what reactions they had to the public. The integrity of the sales

CHEVROLET

Chevrolet has set a new standard of value

With quality that begins in the selection of raw materials and extends to the smallest detail of finish, the new Chevrolet Six has set a new standard for the low-price field. This is not only a new standard of quality, but one of value as well—for this attractive, capable new Six is offered at the lowest prices in Chevrolet history!

Although the new Chevrolet Six is one of the most inexpensive automobiles on the market, it offers fine-car style, performance, comfort and dependability. And along with the economy of a low purchase price, you get the savings of very low operating cost and long life with little upkeep expense.

Consider these many Chevrolet advantages when you buy a low-priced automobile. They mean that the Chevrolet dealer is offering you more motor car quality per dollar in the finest automobile Chevrolet has ever built, at the lowest prices in 20 years of manufacturing!

» **New low prices** «

Roadster, $475; Sport Roadster with rumble seat, $495; Coach or Standard Five-Window Coupe, $545; Phaeton, $510; Standard Coupe, $525; Sport Coupe (rumble seat), $575; Convertible Cabriolet $615; Standard Sedan, $600; Special Sedan, $650. Prices f. o. b. Flint, Mich. Special equipment extra.

The New Chevrolet Convertible Cabriolet—Product of General Motors

NEW CHEVROLET SIX
The Great American Value

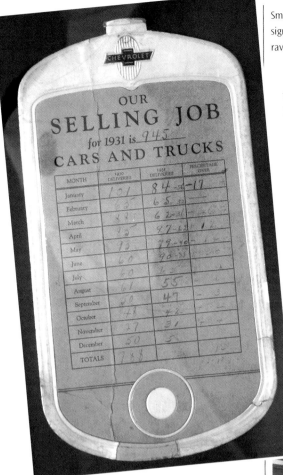

Smith Chevrolet's sales-goal chart for 1931. The many minus signs in the right-hand column reveal the Great Depression's ravages. *Brad Bowling*

OUR SELLING JOB for 1931 is *945* CARS AND TRUCKS

the railroad, and mile marker number zero for the railroad is in the middle of the city at Five Points. They opened Whitehall, which was about two miles south of the center of the city and slightly west. My father ran that until the Depression.

"About 1932 or '33, Chevrolet decided to close Whitehall Chevrolet, and one of my father's proudest accomplishments was that when they liquidated the dealership, there were more assets than debts on the books. They had kept their financial records so sound and so conservative. Around 1938, Chevrolet reopened at that point under [the leadership of] someone else, and after awhile, they had lost their shirts. Chevrolet came looking for my dad to run it. My father and grandfather were able to extract from Chevrolet in writing that my dad would be able to run two places at once in case something ever happened to my grandfather. When my grandfather retired in 1954, my father ran both locations, which just wasn't done at that time. The name of the point at that time was Downtown Chevrolet. I believe it was sold in 1957. I remember taking parts inventory before the sale. He sold it to a man named Tim Timmers. Tim eventually sold the dealership and got another point out on I-85 north of Atlanta."

The economic effects of the Great Depression had been easing for several years before the storm clouds of World War II gathered. When the *New York Times* headline screamed, "WAR," Hal Smith responded.

"I don't remember making a particular preparation in reference to the war," Hal recalls, "but it was a common approach by the dealers to get all the merchandise they could. I rationed cars for the state of Georgia, but the cars we had

department was very important. You didn't make promises you couldn't keep. Mr. Holler was gifted in his phrasing, and he inspired the salesmen and dealers to do a better job.

William Holler's messages got through to the Smith family, and John III picks up the story of the company's exceptional growth through the tough times of the 1930s.

"My dad graduated college in 1926, and in 1927, I think, my grandfather backed him in a satellite Chevrolet dealership, and I think the name of it was Whitehall Chevrolet," John Smith III explains. "That was located on the south side of the center of Atlanta. The center of the city was defined as a place called Five Points. In the '20s, so much evolved and revolved around

NATIONAL AUTOMOBILE DEALERS ASSOCIATION
EMERGENCY NATIONAL COMMITTEE MEETING
JEFFERSON HOTEL, ST. LOUIS, MO. AUGUST 16-17, 1933

John Smith III collection

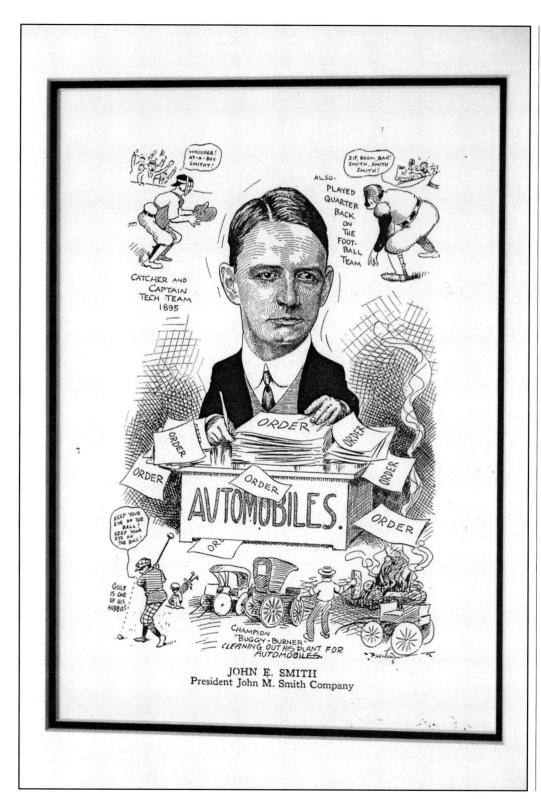

CATCHER AND CAPTAIN TECH TEAM 1895

WHOOPEE! AT-A-BOY SMITHY!

ZIP, BOOM, BAH! SMITH, SMITH SMITH!

ALSO PLAYED QUARTER BACK ON THE FOOT-BALL TEAM

KEEP YOUR EYE ON THE BALL! KEEP YOUR EYE ON THE BALL!

GOLF IS ONE OF HIS HOBBIES

ORDER ORDER ORDER ORDER ORDER ORDER ORDER ORDER

AUTOMOBILES.

CHAMPION "BUGGY-BURNER" CLEANING OUT HIS PLANT FOR AUTOMOBILES.

JOHN E. SMITH
President John M. Smith Company

didn't amount to a hill of beans. We carried out the instructions for the people who wrote the regulations. You couldn't get an automobile if you didn't have the proper authorization. They allowed essential services that were helping in the war effort to have cars—people like doctors [were allowed cars]. There wasn't a lot of rationing because there weren't a lot of cars. The only things [dealerships] had were service and parts. You might have had a few cars to start off, but you couldn't say you were going to make it on the new car business. But parts and service keeping the units running was very important. Who got what was *the* question after the war. There was such a demand for automobiles, and there was a shortage of production at that time. As a result, there was a big demand for automobiles. The demand was so great that people would buy any equipment that was on the automobile, and the more equipment they put on the cars, the more they were going to sell the cars for. The manufacturer passed that on to the dealers, and the dealers passed that on to the customers. We got your automobile for you based on the order that your name came up on the waiting list, but a lot of dealers would move people up the list. The good dealerships were ethical, in that they delivered the automobiles in the order that they were placed on this list."

Today's car enthusiasts are especially attracted to the immediate postwar years. That time period recalls images of optimistic Americans traveling new four-lane highways in jet-age style and purchasing their cars under clear-glass light bulbs at dealerships covered in sweeping neon. After nearly two decades of near-constant uncertainty, America was back. John Smith III began the 1950s as a teenager and took his first steps to become the fourth generation of Smiths in the car business and the third generation in the Chevrolet business.

"I worked in the parts department at Downtown Chevrolet," John III remembers. "It was hot, and my job in my early years was to help store the parts that came in from the delivery trucks. I was just a kid, and my father made me a stock man. In 1954, when I was a little older, I worked as a mechanic's helper, and our job for that summer was to put short blocks into Complete Auto Transit trucks that had burnt-up engines. These trucks were of cab-over construction, and putting short blocks in was a real task! I worked under the trucks, and the mechanic worked in the cab. It took us about four days per short block. That was a hard summer. We must have done eight or ten of those that summer. They were straight sixes. I remember working on the old 216 engines in people's cars as well. I was a tune-up man one year. I remember the huge difference between the 216 and the 235—the real difference being the 216 had a big side panel, and the lifters were mechanical, and we had to lash the valves. You could always tell when you had the engine running right because you'd go around and feel the exhaust. If the exhaust felt right, you knew you had fixed the damn car! Now, the computer tells you, and you'd better hope."

John had joined the family enterprise already knowing the odd day-to-day stories a busy dealership can generate, and the Smith Chevrolet staff brought their individual personalities to work with them.

"We had a body man who was deaf and mute," John recalls. "He was a good body man, and a seemingly really nice guy. I wasn't there for this story, but in the '30s and '40s, the front fenders bolted on to the car like the rear fenders. A body man would get paid in advance based on how much work he had done up to a certain time. This body man must have been hurting for money, but the customer came in, and the manager asked the body man how far along he was at that point. The body man had the fenders hung back on the car, but when the manager opened the hood, the fenders fell off and crashed onto the floor. So much for that big advance!"

Hal Smith (center) receiving his 50-year plaque on July 31, 1977. Presenting the award are (left) Max Young, the southeast's regional manager, Chevrolet Motor Division, and (right) Ed O'Rourke, Atlanta zone manager for Chevrolet. *John Smith III collection*

People sometimes talked about salesmen as if they were a separate race of human beings, and John Smith remembers a few with styles all their own.

"There were some real characters," Smith laughs. "There was a fellow named Slick Stewart. Slick always had a walking cane, and this customer came in with a car that was in pretty bad shape—terribly rusty. Slick took his walking cane and poked a hole right through the rust and said, 'If there was ever a po' som'bitch who needed a trade, it's you!' There aren't many salesmen who'd do that."

Looking back, some of the incidents now make for entertaining memories.

"This was about 1963. We pushed a 1960 Chevrolet into the dead-car stall where we put cars that wouldn't start for the service writer to write up. The back of the building was probably 25 feet off of the ground above a slope. The battery was dead. The porter raised the hood and went to put the charger on the battery, and the car started. It must not have been all the way into park. It went back about 25 feet and hit this big cast-iron radiator that kept it from going through the wall and down

PRESIDENT'S DEALER ADVISORY COUNCIL
LARGE CITY GROUP
JULY 17, 1962

The July 17, 1962, meeting of the President's Dealer Advisory Council's Large City Group. A carryover from the William Holler era, the group took the concerns and ideas of Chevrolet's big-city dealerships to GM's decision makers. A similar group existed for rural and small-town dealers. Hal Smith is seated at the far end of the table, in the center of the three men.
John Smith III collection

that 25-foot drop. The impact knocked the car back into drive, and it went forward, hit a transmission bench, and knocked into a car that was up on a jack and two stands. I didn't see any of this happen, but I saw the radiator, the bench, and the other car. This porter was . . . a really, really nice guy, and all he had done was hook up the battery. I can still hear his voice: 'I didn't do nuthin'!'"

John Smith III graduated from Georgia Tech in 1958. After a few years in the U.S. Navy, he hit the books again and graduated from Harvard Business School in 1962 with an MBA. He received his advanced degree just in time for another period of rapid change for Chevrolet and its market. In the early 1950s, Chrysler President K. T. Keller had been vehemently opposed when he insisted that his

company should keep a line of small, economical cars. As the decade progressed, a fierce little German competitor called Volkswagen threw a scare into America's Big Three and suddenly made Chrysler's Keller look like a prophet and Nash's Rambler Americans and Metropolitans look like strokes of genius. Chevrolet's first effort toward a small car was the loved and hated Corvair.

Celebrating the 100th anniversary of the John Smith Company in 1969. GM president Ed Cole is seen in the center of both photos along with Hal Smith and John Smith III. "In 1964, we added 55,000 square feet to our building and a large indoor showroom that held about 18 or 20 cars," John Smith III remembers. "Inside that showroom, we had a showcase built that housed a buggy and a carriage that my great-grandfather manufactured. The party was held at the then-new Hyatt-Regency in Atlanta. We had about 1,000 people at the party including the mayor and a lot of other prominent dignitaries. Mr. Cole was the featured speaker." *John Smith III collection*

"I drove three years' worth of Corvairs of my own," John reports. "We didn't supply demos to anybody on the staff, including me. I bought my own cars. I had a couple of '62s and a '63, and then I shifted over to Chevelles. The Corvair was not very well received here. It was hard to work on, and it was different to work on, and we had a couple of mechanics who got good at working on them. The problem with the Corvair mechanically was that the aluminum heads or pots would wear out. It was also not easy to tune because it had two carburetors. We never saw the 'Ralph Nader [safety] problems' with them. I drove a lot of them and didn't have any problems with them unless I did something stupid. They were good, sturdy little cars. I was in New England on a ski trip, and I rolled a Corvair on the ice. It had been sleeting, and I wasn't going very fast. I just hit an ice rut, slid down the road, and rolled it over down a little hill. The good news was that it took that accident really well, and the sturdiness of the car surprised me. I used to tell people, 'If you have to hit a tree, the Corvair is the car to hit it with.' That front was accidentally designed to absorb impact before people talked about things like that."

The Chevelle was a more conventional car than the Corvair and a higher quality car than the Chevy II. But in spite of its good qualities, the Chevelle wasn't immune to odd experiences.

"I was doing about 20 miles per hour going over to a storage lot. I'd probably driven that street four or five hundred times, literally. There was a manhole with part of the lip above the pavement. I had just come down a little dip, the car bounced normally, and when it was bouncing back down for the second bounce, it bounced just wrong, and the lip on the manhole caught the cross member. I thought the car had hit a bomb! It was a convertible, and I had my seat belt on, but the guy riding with me didn't, and he hit the convertible top with his head. I really thought somebody had blown the car up. It knocked the oil pan out. It really was like you were riding along, and suddenly, *BOOM*, like somebody put dynamite under you."

As the 1960s progressed, millions of baby boomers hit the dealerships looking for something youthful and exciting. The Big Three all noticed customers buying small economy cars for a reasonable base price and then buying everything on the option list, thus making it a luxury car. To tap this market, Ford's answer was the Mustang. Two years later, Chevrolet responded with the Camaro. By the close of the decade, a Camaro could be had as a sporty economy car or a 400-horsepower heavyweight.

To my good friend
Hal Smith
Best wishes for
your continued
success
Ed Cole

"The Camaro was pretty well received. That was a popular car. We had sold three Camaros in one weekend. We called for a few more Camaros, and at that time the allotments were all done by hand. The man I was ordering from said, 'I hate to tell you this, John, but the Camaro plant just went on strike this morning.' The Camaro plant went down for something like 150 or 180 days. Ordering cars was different in those days. By that time, we were not ordering nearly as many cars as we had been in earlier days because we were stocking more cars, but we still couldn't restock the lot to make up for the Camaros we had just sold. I also remember the special orange pace car which had the 396 engine in it. The problem for the South was that the pace car model didn't have air conditioning, so it was not a great piece of merchandise for this part of the country."

The early 1970s delivered the gas crunch and strange economic times to the American car dealer, and Smith Chevrolet did not escape them. John Smith mentions the gas crunch only as a challenge, because his attention was dominated by the other difficulties of that time.

"We had always prided ourselves in pricing our service labor at the lower end of the range and getting lots of volume," John explains. "Unfortunately, when the wage and price controls

John Smith III in 1969. *John Smith III collection*

Smith Chevrolet seems to have had a knack for retaining employees. Captain John Smith is located in the center, along with longtime sales manager Barney Stodghill (left) and Wesley Slate (right). Slate would later become the company's general manager when Hal Smith took the helm. *John Smith III collection*

hit, we were caught with a low labor rate, and we could not raise our prices when we needed to. It was a problem when we tried to recruit mechanics. We were able to provide enough work to keep our people happy. We decided it wasn't worth the hassle to try and fight the government on it if we could just outlast them. It went on about 18 months. It was a disaster. The other stunner was the price inflation upon the announcement of the 1974 vehicles in the fall of '73. The MSRP (Manufacturers Suggested Retail Price) on our bread-and-butter cars went from about $3,500 to about $4,500. If I remember right, it went up something like $970. That's what I call sticker shock! GM raised the prices several times during the '73 year, and they added features to the cars to try and make you think you were getting something for that additional money. When the customer is looking at the sticker on the window, he doesn't care how the prices got like that. People about fainted! The fall of '73 was the deadest fish I ever saw. There were no customers, and 1974 was the most difficult year I spent in the car business until 1991."

Smith Chevrolet was sold in the mid-1990s after 130 years in the vehicle business, but Hal Smith passes along advice that will never fade in value.

"My father ran a very good business and a very ethical business. Some of the dealers overpriced after the war, and some of them took money under the table to get a car, and my father wasn't involved in any of that. The truth of the matter is that the unethical didn't last long because they were not top-notch business folks. It's probably the same today."

127

Dimmitt Chevrolet

Two views of Dimmitt Chevrolet in Clearwater, Florida, show the used-car lot before and after World War II. Dimmitt appears to have been another dealership that lacked participation in the OK Used Cars program at that time. Larry Dimmitt Sr. was born in 1880 and started in the vehicle business with a Buick dealership and distributorship. He also sold Peerless and Liberty automobiles and White trucks in Savannah, Georgia. The economic slump after World War I made the Florida land boom of the 1920s attractive to Dimmitt, and he fell in love with the village of Clearwater, where he simply walked into the Ford dealership and offered to buy the place. Dimmitt handled Ford until 1933. Thanks to the rapid development of land in the area, Ford tractors did well. But Dimmitt was dissatisfied with some Ford policies of the time and switched to Chevrolet. *Dimmitt Chevrolet collection*

Larry Dimmitt Jr., wearing a coat and tie, was born in 1914 and is seen here with longtime Dimmitt service department manager Walker Brewer circa 1950. "We had to do service work during the Second World War because there weren't any cars to sell," Larry Dimmitt Jr. remembers. "[Even after the war], the procurement of parts in the '40s wasn't easy. The car would sit there for weeks jacked up. We even had parts flown in. My neighbor, Quinlin Chevrolet, had a huge building just for parts, and he took orders for them. We all scratched out a living." *Dimmitt Chevrolet collection*

"We had a thriving body shop," Larry Dimmitt Jr. says. "All these retired winter visitors came down here, and they didn't have anything to do with their time, so they ran into each other. We did a lot of insurance work." *Dimmitt Chevrolet collection*

The Dimmitt Chevrolet showroom for the 1963 season. *Dimmitt Chevrolet collection*

Dimmitt Chevrolet's service department in the early 1960s. *Dimmitt Chevrolet collection*

129

MANDEVILLE CHEVROLET—NORTH ATTLEBORO, MASSACHUSETTS

Chevrolet's First Lady?

Ephram Mandeville was subjected to poisonous gas in the trenches of World War I. The resulting lung ailments finally took his life in 1929, leaving his wife, Donia, alone with three small children to support. The stock market crashed a few months later, throwing Manville, Rhode Island, and the rest of the United States into the jaws of the Great Depression and making the Mandeville's family business virtually impossible to sell. With no one to buy the business and no way to support herself and her children, Donia Mandeville took over where her husband left off, and by accident, she may have become the first woman to sign on as dealer-operator of a General Motors franchise.

Donia's oldest child, Fernand, stepped into the business when he grew up. Two of Fernand's

The innkeeper was honored to have such a distinguished guest. The road could be hot and dusty, or cold and icy, depending on the time of year, and in either circumstance, the hotel was a good place to stop. Owner and guest talked. Maybe they shared small talk about weather or maybe took part in deep discussions of current events and an uncertain future. Shoe buckles were still the fashion of the day, and the two men admired each other's buckles. After some talk, they decided to swap shoe buckle sets. This was how George Washington's shoe buckles came to be displayed in North Attleboro Massachusetts, only to be stolen a few years later.

A little girl named Sarah Orne once played in the North Attleboro streets. She didn't know that over 200 years later, people would be driving powerful, horseless machines over a street named for her. Orne Street connects U.S. 1 to its older alignment, U.S. 1A. Freedom was in the air in the young United States, and in some ways, it served as a catalyst for North America's Industrial Revolution. Some of the credit goes to Paul Revere, whose "midnight ride" is celebrated in history, legend, and poetry and whose industrial innovations in silversmithing, copper plating, and currency printing are in use to this day. Revere married Sarah Orne in 1757, and she bore him eight children before her death at age 37.

That early industrial revolution spread west into northern Rhode Island's Blackstone River Valley where the giant textile-producing Manville Jenks Mill spawned the village of Manville.

Donia Mandeville took over a business in Manville, Rhode Island, and moved it to North Attleboro, which apparently made her the first woman to sign on as dealer-operator of a Chevrolet franchise.

children, Ron and Lucille, still proudly run the business their grandfather started and their grandmother ran. As children, they watched the business move from the water-powered heavy manufacturing town of Manville through the apple orchards and family farms to North Attleboro, Massachusetts. Mandeville Chevrolet stands on U.S. 1, the former main artery between Boston and Providence.

"Manville, Rhode Island, was a fairly substantial textile town along the Blackstone River," Ron Mandeville tells. "I'm pretty sure they supplied material to make war goods as early as the turn of the [twentieth] century. It was heavily populated by French Canadians, and there were sections of town with other immigrants like other villages in New England. The majority of the people worked at the Manville Jenks Mill, which was the main employer. Manville was probably a couple of thousand people at its height, and most of them worked at the mill with the rest of the population catering to the mill. The mill itself built row houses to house the workers, and I remember my father telling me stories of the early days of the dealership when people who worked at the mill each had an envelope containing the few dollars they

Upon his return from World War I, Ephram Mandeville founded Mandeville Garage in the textile-mill town of Manville, Rhode Island. His building at 141 Railroad Street handled the occasional Chevrolet sale, serving as a satellite to a larger Bowtie dealership in the city of Woonsocket. The young, handsome, promising Mandeville had been seriously injured by poison gases during the war, and he succumbed to his lung ailments in 1929, leaving his wife, Donia, to face the Great Depression with three small children and a dealership to support. Donia Mandeville rose to the challenge and is believed to be the first woman to actively own and operate a General Motors franchise. *Mandeville Chevrolet collection*

Donia Mandeville and her three children—Fernand, Ruth, and Rachel—in 1933. Other women had inherited dealerships upon their husbands' passing, but nearly all turned the businesses over to their sons or hired managers. With her children too young to assume responsibility and her dealership too small to turn over to anyone else, Donia Mandeville ran all aspects of the dealership herself. Her son, Fernand Mandeville, later became the dealer-operator of Mandeville Chevrolet in the 1950s. *Mandeville Chevrolet collection*

A delivery of 1936 Chevrolets arrives at Mandeville Chevrolet. *Mandeville Chevrolet collection*

interaction," Ron Mandeville continues. "I know my grandparents sold Mobil gas, and they were a Firestone tire dealer. They did towing, and they repaired cars, primarily. I believe it was called Mandeville Garage. By 1922, the business grew into being a satellite dealer for Marcoux Chevrolet in Woonsocket, Rhode Island, which was the closest larger city to Manville. Marcoux Chevrolet was a fairly substantial Chevrolet point, and they allowed us to sell cars in Manville under some satellite agreement. It was a very small concrete building on the main drag, Railroad Street, which ran along the Blackstone River and the railroad tracks that used to supply the textile mill. The dealership was probably a mile from the mill, and that's where they started selling Chevrolet. I guess that agreement lasted about four or five years, and they eventually got their own franchise. I hear that it was a very meager existence. My grandfather was self-taught

made at the mill that week—a dollar for food, 50 cents toward the car. People were on very strict envelope budgets. It was not a big, affluent town even through it was not too far from some big cities. It was very, very much outside the Providence/Boston influence, which was one of the things that led Chevrolet to recommend [in the 1960s] that we not stay in that town. There was no chance for growth there."

Lucille Mandeville contends that northern Rhode Island's French Canadians were the adventurous ones in their families. They had left the safety of large, established family farms in Canada for the adventure and chance to succeed that the United States offered. Like many who settled in Manville for a more interesting life, Ephram Mandeville didn't stay in the mills long and gravitated to the established, but still young and exciting, automobile business.

"My grandfather came back from the war and wanted some kind of mechanical/automobile

A pair of Mandeville Chevrolet mechanics and a couple of their buddies check out the new Chevrolets in 1940. *Mandeville Chevrolet collection*

Fernand Mandeville opens the door to Chevrolet's first truly new postwar model at a special promotional event—probably the 1949 announcement day. Standing with him is Mandeville Chevrolet salesman Paul Gingras, who also served as Deputy Chief of Police for the neighboring city of Lincoln, Rhode Island. *Mandeville Chevrolet collection*

at everything. They were self-sufficient. He pretty much did everything—fixing tires, pumping gas, fixing cars—and on the occasions when someone actually had enough money to buy a car, he sold cars. It was a one- or two-man show with long days and hard work, not a lot of glamour like now. My grandfather dealt with the wooden wheels. We complain now about brake shudder and suspension problems we have today, but they were dealing with wooden wheels where no two wheels were really the same, with solid rubber tires that had no life expectancy beyond a few thousand miles. These were all stories of keeping the cars going—putting Band-Aids on tops of Band-Aids to keep people moving."

Ron is charmed by the thought of the atmosphere that must have filled Mandeville Garage.

"When my grandfather was working the filling station in the '20s, the boys would roll

Donia Mandeville closes a sale at her desk in 1951. Note that the customers don't mind sealing the deal right in the service bay of Mandeville Chevrolet. *Mandeville Chevrolet collection*

into the station on Saturday nights with their dates, and they would say, 'Fill it up!' but they would hold five fingers outside the door, meaning to only put 50 cents worth of gas in. This way, the boys would sound like big shots to their girlfriends, making it look like they were big spenders with some dough, and all the while, they'd be giving hand signals that they only had 50 cents on them."

The Roaring Twenties ended and the Great Depression began. Ephram Mandeville passed away, and Donia found herself alone at the helm of the Chevrolet franchise in a struggling town.

"It all started to change in the late '20s, and that's why it's surprising to me that when my grandfather passed away in '29 my grandmother stuck with it," Ron relates. "Things were changing. We'd had the stock market crash, and the

car business was changing to where we had bigger, better, stronger cars and trucks. There were starting to be a lot more trucks sold to move America. You would have thought that my grandmother would have passed on all that and let a man's world, as it was back then, take over, but she decided she wanted to be the dealer, and in 1930, she did become the dealer in the original location in Manville. She went through

Fernand Mandeville poses in a 1953 Corvette promotional car on tour with the Chevrolet Dealers Association. *Mandeville Chevrolet collection*

all the changes and growth of Chevrolet and General Motors. Her husband passed away, and she decided to become a businesswoman at a time when the town she lived in was not a liberal, fast-moving place."

An exhausted America hauled its load through the Thirsty Thirties, and as the seemingly endless Great Depression refused to loosen its grip, young Fernand began to ease into the dealership chores.

"My father felt a lot of pity when people dipped into that envelope to make their car payments," Ron says, his recollection of his father's sadness coming through his voice nearly 70 years later. "Sometimes he wasn't there in time, and most of the money was gone. He felt for the people and felt bad that he was the one getting sent out there to pick the money up. People would look at him, look down in the envelope, and look back at him, and sometimes, there wasn't enough. My father had that feeling that everybody was letting everybody else down, but they were all in the same boat, and everybody knew that times were tough."

Donia Mandeville receiving her 25-year award from her Chevrolet zone manager in 1955. *Mandeville Chevrolet collection*

As was so common with dealerships that survived the Depression, non-monetary, this-for-that agreements got dealers and customers through the day. They couldn't solve the Depression, but they could handle it.

"There were some barter stories," Ron recounts. "My grandmother was a one-person show like my grandfather was before he died. My father told me that when he was young, he would help her reconcile the checkbook and keep track of who owed what on the revolving charge account that she let people set up. She

had a little bit of money—maybe a little more than other people—but she spread it around to keep everybody going. This went a long way toward building up the trust and reputation that we still benefit from today. They used to re-groove worn-out tires with a special tool and send the customer on his way, and if he could pay, great, but if he couldn't pay, it didn't matter, because someday, they'd make it up. She did everything she needed to do to keep it going and not fail at a time when she would have had plenty of excuses to fail.

"Manville had an Italian neighborhood, and they had an Enrico Caruso club for the great Italian tenor. The club members would get repairs, and instead of paying money, they would feed the entire dealership—something like spaghetti and meatballs on Monday and fish and chips on Friday and during Lent. A lot of the people who worked in the mill would trade material that my grandmother could make a dress or blanket out of. There really wasn't a lot to barter, unfortunately. It was a poor town. There was no livestock because it was an industrial town, so

Above and next page: Mandeville Chevrolet's days in Manville, Rhode Island, were numbered. General Motors was quickly realizing that the small industrial town was not going to grow at the necessary rate to support the dealership. With great pain, Fernand Mandeville agreed to move the dealership eight miles to North Attleboro, Massachusetts, in 1964. *Mandeville Chevrolet collection*

they didn't get cows in trade for cars or tires, but there were cases when a guy who was a carpenter would fix a door in exchange for repairs. My grandmother couldn't afford a new overhead door for the shop, and the carpenter couldn't afford to get his car fixed, so they'd trade. If there was a trade that was needed, they made it work. That, and her compassion for fronting people on things when they couldn't afford it, benefited her later when things got good after the Second World War. She had the reputation

for having been there when things were bad, and people seemed to think she should get her just rewards when things were good."

Donia Mandeville's children were teenagers when the war cries in Europe burst forth into grave reality and the cars stopped coming to the dealerships.

The 1940s were underway in earnest, and Mandeville Chevrolet started hoarding cars and fast-moving parts. Before the cars were cut off completely, car-hauling truckers were already

being cut back, and Mandeville Chevrolet would go to Tarrytown, New York, to pick cars up directly from the plant.

"They also used to pick up cars at the port of Rhode Island in all kinds of weather," Ron Mandeville tells. "Little did the customers know the cars had been halfway to hell driving them back from New York to Rhode Island before they were sold as brand-new cars."

Like all nightmares, World War II ended, the waiting-list shenanigans slowed down, new

models and exciting announcement days dazzled the showrooms, and the 1950s began. Prewar America had been erased, and the bold, new jet age had emerged, bringing radical changes and new products to Chevrolet showrooms, much to the frustration of those whose norms were formed before the war. Ron Mandeville tells of Powerglide.

"We had a mechanic we called Joe B. who swore up and down that automatic transmissions would never be any good. Try as he might, he could never talk anybody out of the fact that there wasn't going to be three pedals in the car. The old-time mechanics had quite a bit of doom and gloom to them. They were probably just as suspicious of Powerglide as we are of adding more computers to a car now. If an automatic had some minor problems, they'd say, 'Ha, I told you they weren't going to be any good!' Now, automatics are in just about everything, but early on, the [pre-1953] Powerglides weren't that good. You used to rev the heck out of them, and you'd just sit there."

Mandeville Chevrolet benefited from the postwar boom years, as did all dealerships, with some regionally unique characteristics. Manville was a solidly blue-collar town, but soldiers returned from the war with a gritty sense of independence. With the GI Bill helping to pay for education, going to the mill every day to work for someone else became unacceptable to many of them. The ex-soldiers and others started businesses. They worked as carpenters and plumbers, painters and electricians. And they needed trucks. General Motors made truck styling a priority and introduced the beautiful Advance Design bodies in late 1947. They soon sported five-window cabs with trim and comfort options. Chevrolet and GMC trucks may have looked basically the same on the surface, but underneath it all, the two were quite different. Chevrolet trucks still had drivetrains with splash engine oiling, babbit rod bearings, enclosed driveshafts, wooden-bed floors, and extremely low gear ratios, while GMCs sported

Mandeville Chevrolet moved to its new facilities in North Attleboro, Massachusetts, in time for the announcement of the 1965 models. Fernand Mandeville is seen here with a special 1965 Chevrolet Chevelle cutaway car that levitated off its chassis at a push of a button to reveal all the car's mechanical features. Ron Mandeville remembers the car being an attractive metallic green and says the local high-school auto-shop teacher brought the class to the dealership to examine the inside of the unique car. *Mandeville Chevrolet collection*

high-pressure oiling, insert bearings, automatic transmissions, open drive shafts, better highway gear ratios, and all-steel beds. Clear into the 1960s, GMCs were available with higher-performance Pontiac engines for four-speed Hydra-Matic transmissions. As a result, they came with a much higher price tag. In some ways, Chevrolet's deficiencies worked to Mandeville Chevrolet's advantage.

"I get the impression that a half-ton or three-quarter-ton GMC was much more truck than a Chevrolet in content," Mandeville contemplates. "The idea persisted into the 1970s when, by that time, they were both built on the same assembly line from the same exact components. On the other hand, I think we might have benefited from not having as sophisticated a vehicle with our Chevrolet trucks because we had a very price-sensitive market, and I think it helped to have any dollar advantage over the competition, even if it meant people were driving with a 20-year-old drivetrain in the 1950s. Part of our success story is that we were selling Chevrolets and not Cadillacs or Lincolns. We had the blue-collar man's vehicle in a blue-collar community. The frustration comes at the end of that story [in the 1970s] when, for so long the GMCs had been better, even though they were built on the same lines, people still thought the Chevrolets were less capable trucks. Today, I see General Motors going toward what they're calling Professional Grade with the GMC truck,

trying to get back to that and play on that history. To some degree, General Motors is trying to differentiate between our two brands and maybe get back to a two-tiered system because there's really no reason to sell the exact same trucks against each other."

All Chevrolet dealers remember the 1955 announcement fondly. Chevrolet went from being the economy car driven through the mud to work to the swank, two-tone highway performer. It was a new and exciting V-8-powered product with snap and style in no way tied to the past. Even in six-cylinder form, the 1955 Chevrolet had flash and dash, beginning the three-year stretch so beloved by modern car restorers. Ron Mandeville was born when the Hot Ones premiered in the showrooms.

"The timing of the '55 introduction and the timing of the growth in the area hit us pretty well, but I heard my father telling stories that the 1957 Chevrolet hardly sold brand new, although it was one of the best-selling used cars in automotive history. To this day, it's one of the hottest-selling used cars there's ever been. The styling had gone a little too far past its mark, and its styling was radical enough that it made people go look at the '57 Fords instead. I think it all goes back to the rush to put fins on all the cars and clocks in all the dashes, and they came to market [with something that wasn't right for the market]. My father spoke fondly of them because they sold so well as used cars, but he couldn't sell one new for love nor money. People were asking to buy his personal '56 Chevrolet after they saw the '57s. In those days, announcement day was when they had all the windows in the showrooms waxed up well in advance. No magazines had preview pictures of the cars in them. The car used to show up on the tractor trailer truck covered. We used to be like FBI or CIA agents, keeping all the cars covered up and not letting anybody get any view of anything. They had a lot of expectation of selling the '57 Chevrolets, and they didn't sell. Chevrolet was shocked, but history being what it is, they came back as one of the best-selling used cars in Mandeville Chevrolet history."

It wasn't long before Mandeville Chevrolet had another product that generated mixed feelings. The Corvair was introduced in 1960.

"That was another Joe B.–doubting car. He was still around, although old. My father always had the impression that Chevrolet was on the right track with the Corvair, that having weight over the rear wheels in the wind and snow was the right thing to do. My mother had one of the first ones. We had a lot of trouble with the carburetor and fuel systems in that car, and my mother was a little mad at Chevrolet for trying new technology on her. My mother didn't like being the guinea pig for the Corvair, and she thought that if she had one, other people would want them, and if they lacked success with theirs, they might say, 'We got one because Mrs. Mandeville had one.'"

A sadness swept over the family when General Motors said Mandeville Chevrolet would have to move.

"That was when Chevrolet indicated to my father that Manville, although fine for conducting some kinds of business, was not going to be a good growth area and was not on the main thoroughfares that would bring great success," Mandeville remembers. "I think Chevrolet thought enough of my grandmother and my father to say they were too good to stay in this little town and tried to make them think about getting out. They were very hesitant and against moving out. They figured the town had stuck with us though the tough times, and we should stay with the town. I know my father agonized when the realization came that Chevrolet was right that there was no future in Manville, Rhode Island, and he was going to leave the people who had given us our existence.

"In 1963, the decision was made to move to North Attleboro, Massachusetts, and buy Wright Chevrolet. The move was only eight miles, but it might as well have been another country as far as my grandmother and father felt. They'd had great success in their hometown, and they were worried that if they moved to another state, people would not follow and

Fernand Mandeville and son Ron with a promotional Corvette in 1989. *Mandeville Chevrolet collection*

they might not accepted in the new community. They went through a lot of trials over it, but one thing they had was very good guidance from Chevrolet. We would probably not be in existence if we had not moved. North Attleboro is on the main route between Boston and Providence, and we have I-95 nearby, which is the main route up and down the East Coast, and we're right on Route 1.

"We got very good information from Chevrolet and the zone managers of the time. Manville was not on a major route, but people found us, and things were starting to grow. Attleboro is a big jewelry town, and the postwar growth was pushing at the seams to get more

stuff from more outlets. That's what led Chevrolet to say to us, 'Hey, we like what you're doing, and you're really aggressive, but you're in a non-growth town.' [It seemed like] we might have been cutting into the sales of other dealerships, including the dealer in Woonsocket we had once been part of. I think some of the dealers might have been complaining about little old Mandeville Chevrolet taking some of their business. They weren't just whining, but rather, they were making the point that there were too many dealers in too small an area, and Chevrolet, to their credit, had enough loyalty to us to acknowledge that we were doing a good job but in the wrong place. We were kind of nervous at first because we weren't sure if we were going to be accepted in the new community because we had displaced a local fixture—Wright Chevrolet. [By the late 1960s], we were accepted, and we had much more affluent customers wanting to do business with us, and we finally had the community to match what was available from the General—the SS Camaros, Z28s, 396 Chevelles, and luxury Caprices."

The move to North Attleboro in 1964 coincided with Chevrolet's introduction of the Chevelle, and this lead to one of Mandeville Chevrolet's greatest displays.

"I think there's some truth to the idea that [the Chevelle was the return of the '55 Chevrolet in terms of size, weight, price, and features]. When we moved from Rhode Island in '64, it was more prevalent for General Motors to have a lot of say in how we did things, and they had a big hand in getting us established in North Attleboro. We had a '64 Chevelle cutaway car that came from Detroit for our grand opening at the new place. The car body went up and down on its chassis so you could see the whole chassis and drivetrain, and there were cutaway segments so you could see all the suspension. I remember we had all the high-school auto-shop kids come to the dealership to see the '64 Chevelle cutaway car on display. I want to say it was green. I think they also sent an engine on a stand that was a cutaway [so you could see all the parts inside] at shows."

The adolescent Ron Mandeville was stirred by the introduction of the Camaro in 1967, excited that Chevrolet had produced a heavier duty, true muscle car. A few years later, this excitement turned to embarrassment as circumstances forced America into fuel-efficient thinking.

"We had been on South Washington Street right in downtown North Attleboro, but we bought the land on Route 1 in 1969," Ron remembers. "On September 14, 1973, we moved to Route 1, where we are to this day, and we had a big grand opening. I helped move the parts department and the inventory. We had 10 or 12 four-barrel 350 Caprice station wagons with the woodgrain on them. Then the gas lines hit, and it was almost like you were un-American if you had those cars, and we were almost hiding those cars and pointing, as an alternative, to the Vega Kammback station wagons and Vega GTs. We thought we had the answer when the gas crunch hit with the Vega, but unfortunately, almost everybody we put into one suffered some kind of trouble because of poor design or poor execution of the plan.

"Did we make more enemies than friends with the Vega? Well, the jury's still out, but I'm afraid we may have made as many enemies as friends. The Vega didn't have to be a fancy, highfalutin answer, but it at least had to be a competent, not-make-matters-worse answer. We were practically embarrassed to have the 350 Caprice wagons, and we recommended the Vega, but the Vega bombarded the service department and left us with some upset people. We got burned when we could have been grabbing a whole new market before the imports got it. Down the street from us, Datsun and Toyota had moved into what had been small used-car lots, and of course, we laughed and said no one in his right mind would buy one of those. Then the Vega came out, and it was a small car, but at least it was made by General Motors. I had the misfortune of seeing my father selling a Vega to my cousin and his wife, and they had an overheating problem, a warped head, and every other problem you could have with a Vega.

"Ford, unfortunately, had the same scenario with Pinto. America had Pinto, Omni, and Vega, and there was something flawed in every one of them. I remember myself stopping on I-295 when I saw a Vega broke down, and there was an oil pressure sensor that would shut the engine off if the oil pressure got too low. The electrical plugs used to fall out of those. I plugged it back in, the car started, and the people thought I was a marvel.

"The [Japanese cars] didn't offer much, but they didn't have as many flaws. The Japanese cars rusted out faster than our cars at that time, but mechanically, they ran fine.

"What I remember about Vega was the feeling that we let down the public when we attempted to come out with something different. To this day, the family still feels repercussions over what was inflicted on trusting, unsuspecting buyers. Maybe it's worse in our situation because they trusted our judgment, and we had trusted GM to have a better mousetrap. On the other hand, we sold a lot of them because, I think, it was a Chevrolet alternative in getting a small car. When the gas crunch really hit, we were at least sitting there with something, but the question is, was it with the right thing?"

The turbulence of the 1970s ended, and Mandeville Chevrolet settled into the corporate norms of the 1980s and 1990s. Fernand Mandeville passed away in the 1990s and left his children, Ron and Lucille, at the helm. There's some indication that Lucille's children may follow in the family footsteps. The Mandevilles are all living the legacy of a man who gave his life for the American military in the Great War and the woman who rose to the occasion of being one of the auto industry's earliest female dealers.

"We were fairly close, and we lived in the same house with her in my early years," Ron Mandeville says. "I looked up greatly to my grandmother, as did my sister, Lucille. My grandmother was a very forceful, smart role model for people. She had a young family of three children, the oldest of which was only five or six years old. She had a lot of reasons to give up early on, but here we are."

CULBERSON-STOWERS CHEVROLET—PAMPA, TEXAS

Dust, War, and Oil

"Not many people have the opportunity to work with their fathers, and certainly, not many people have the opportunity to work with their grandfathers. The dealership environment has a family orientation. I had the opportunity to work with my grandfather for 13 years, and he was wonderful," says Richard Stowers of his maternal grandfather who bought a Chevrolet dealership during the Texas Panhandle's mildly prosperous 1920s, only to have it run over by the Dust Bowl a few years later.

Frank Morgan Culberson was born in 1895. He was the middle child, but he was called Big Brother by his sisters because he was known for taking care of them all. He continued to care for his family as he raised his daughter, Dorothy, "Dot" to her friends, and until Dot married Dick Stowers and they had a son, Richard. At age 94, Frank Culberson was still working in the dealership that had been his for over 60 years. He died just two months after he retired from his lifelong career. He left Dick, Dot, and Richard to tell the story of the Chevrolet dealership that dug itself out from under the Dust Bowl and survived.

Culberson had put his few years of college education to work as a bank examiner in Santa Fe, New Mexico, but he lost his job as the political parties changed during an election year. While he was working in Santa Fe, Culberson met T. F. Smalling. After being let go from his job, Culberson returned to Texas and went into business with Smalling. The two joined the insurance industry.

"Daddy always said that if it hadn't been for his banking experience, they never would have made it," Dot tells. "In 1927, they were selling insurance in Borger, Texas, and when they were here in Pampa, they saw the Chevrolet dealership for sale. They were driving a 1925 Chevrolet, in fact. They started home, and in the middle of the trip, they turned around, came back, and bought the dealership from Mr. Butler. They borrowed some money from the First National Bank in Pampa, and the only

The Dust Bowl's defining storm slowly and quietly envelops the Texas Panhandle on April 14, 1935. Culberson-Smalling Chevrolet survived and became Culberson-Stowers Chevrolet in the 1950s. *White Deer Land Museum collection*

142

A lady strolled out of the afternoon church service in her white Sunday dress. In minutes, she would be running and her dress would be brown. An out-of-work farmhand counted his pocket change and pondered how many meals he could get out of his life savings of $2.46. "Maybe them Reds are right." He didn't see what was coming.

A man was getting ready for his night job and changing into his work clothes. He had put one shoe on and was reaching for the other when, all of a sudden, he found he couldn't see. He sat terrified. He remembered a few neighbors who had gone blind on bad Prohibition liquor, but he had never touched the stuff. He then realized his room had gone dark in the afternoon.

A minister comforted the members of his afternoon congregation, saying the end of the world was upon them.

The sky went black in Amarillo, Texas, at 3:50 P.M. Pampa, Texas, experienced the same things at 4:50 P.M.

The land in western Oklahoma and the Texas Panhandle had been plowed and grazed, square mile after square mile, baring and loosening the soil. The weather conditions of Sunday, April 14, 1935, were not unusual, but they were extreme. A long drought had sucked the life out of a region already suffering from the Great Depression. Winds from the south routinely scream across the Texas Panhandle prairie in the spring, but the winds of the Dust Bowl's defining storm were not especially strong. Usually, the wind kicked up and the dust followed, but this time, the dust came first. The 200-foot-tall wall of gentle violence looked alive—rolling, boiling, crawling, and enveloping. It wasn't the first storm of the Dust Bowl, nor the last, but it was the worst. The dust rolled north, covering houses from eastern New Mexico to the Dakotas, choking cattle to death, and trapping people in their homes and they sat with wet towels over their heads. The poor, living in tarpapered box homes, watched the dust pour through the cracks before it became too dark to see. Even in finer homes, the dust seemed to penetrate, inundating clothing stored in closed drawers and wardrobes.

In Pampa, Love's Cafe kept the candles lit as alarmed citizens tried to calm themselves with coffee and conversation. A. D. Kirk got out of his car when the sky went black and felt his way along the curb until he felt a driveway he thought was his, and once inside turned on his electric lights. The dust was so thick he still couldn't see anything. Stories of the resulting poverty played out in John Steinbeck's Grapes of Wrath and Woody Guthrie's "Great Dust Storm." Midwesterners told each other that so-and-so had died from "dust pneumony." People struggled to save up the $10 it took to buy enough gasoline to get to California. Many felt they had no choice but to cut an old car down into a truck and head west on U.S. 66.

The Work Progress Administration planted 217 million trees on 30,000 farms in long stands called "shelter belts" to shield the dry soil from the wind, and new techniques of terraced farming have kept the Dust Bowl from repeating itself. The Texas Panhandle's oil industries flourished again by the late 1940s, and the bad times quickly faded into old memories.

Frank Culberson was the kind of man who sheltered his family from his worries. He didn't tell his family his thoughts when the stock market crashed in 1929, and he didn't take his dust-generated troubles home in the 1930s. He didn't spend hours telling his grandchildren how he kept his Chevrolet dealership's doors open for the Pampa, Texas, public through the trials of the Great Depression, the Dust Bowl, and the shortages of World War II. He just worked hard and did it without the complaints or bragging that today's historians would love to hear.

We don't know the details of the dealership's Dust Bowl survival. All we know it that Culberson-Stowers Chevrolet still serves Pampa, even after having survived those times. As a stoic Midwestern rancher would say, "Nuf said."

time the bank was ever robbed was the next day after they had borrowed the money."

By the early 1930s, Culberson was a married man with children depending on him, but ever the pillar of strength, he shielded his family from his business worries, leaving them and historians to wonder how he made it through the Great Depression and the Dust Bowl's consequences. It took $450 to $750 to buy a Chevrolet, with a down payment of one-third and the rest owed in 12 to 18 months. The monthly payments came to about $40. This was all after the oil boom started in the fall of 1926. The dealership had a repossession day in 1931 to raise money to pay off the bank. Culberson was proud of never having missed a payroll.

As the Depression eased and memories of the Dust Bowl blew away, times turned for the better. The *Pampa News* reported in a 1941 edition that Culberson-Smalling Chevrolet had sold over 16,000 vehicles between 1927 and 1941 and that for five of those years, the dealership had grossed over $1 million each year. Despite all the booms and busts, the dealership had gone from 15 employees in 1927 to 43 in 1941. Culberson bought out Smalling in 1941.

The shortages of World War II set in, and like all dealerships, Culberson-Smalling Chevrolet depended on the service department to keep busy through the crisis.

"They had to make it on used cars," Dot tells. "They had to do a lot of traveling to find used cars to bring home and sell. I think they went as far as Denver for them and came back in caravans. They also made it with service because the people had to keep their cars going."

The war ended, and the United States woke up to the sunny morning of the twentieth century's postwar prosperity. While many American children of the 1930s grew up in poverty, their generation is often envied for having reached their prime of life in the prosperous bliss of the 1950s. Kansas City, Missouri, native Dick Stowers was in the right place at the right time.

"My dad was a company doctor for Ford Motor Company, so we drove Fords most of the time," Dick Stowers remembers. "We always had a bigger car also, and I remember Pierce-Arrows, LaSalles, Buicks, and Cadillacs. Cars didn't interest me much at that time. I had never driven a Chevrolet regularly until I met Dot."

In 1950, Dick Stowers may not have been taken with automobiles, but he was enamored with Dot Culberson. The two began dating. Stowers' future father in-law liked him and invited him to work in the dealership. Stowers started in the parts department, moved on to the service department, and was in sales by 1953.

Dick and Dot were married just in time for the introduction of the Powerglide. With its Dynaflow characteristics and the Chevrolet six having only a fraction of the power of its Buick eight cousins to power it, the Powerglide had a reputation for being painfully slow in the rapidly advancing area of postwar acceleration. But on the Texas Panhandle's open roads and generally flat countryside, the Powerglide Chevrolet's far better rear-axle ratio let these little economy cars glide along like their much more expensive relatives. Powerglide was the right thing for the region.

"We had several Powerglide Chevrolets of our own, one after the other in the early '50s," Dick Stowers remembers. "They were fun cars. [The early Powerglides didn't shift], and we had a lot of trouble convincing people to get into one instead of a standard shift. They weren't sure they wanted the automatic. Now, Culberson used to own the Olds-Cadillac dealership as well—a separate dealership that he bought, I think, in 1946—and they already had the Hydra-Matic by '46. The Powerglide was smooth—a nice transmission—and a lot of people liked it because of the smoothness. They were slower than the Hydra-Matics. If

you were trying to compete with someone taking off from a stop sign, you'd have trouble. When they went to [the shifting Powerglide in 1953] and the V-8 engine in '55, it made a big difference for the Powerglide and for Chevrolet. People were delighted on test drives with automatic transmissions and power steering, but they used to ask, 'Will it go out?'"

Engines and transmissions are the married couples of the automotive world, and Dick's memories of the early Powerglides are coupled with his memories of the same era's powerplants.

"We had trouble with the engines in the '50s. They used oil. We found we couldn't use

Above: T. F. Smalling (left) and the dapper Frank Culberson enjoy a cigarette break on a Texas sidewalk. "Daddy always said that if it hadn't been for his banking experience, they never would have made it," Dot Stowers tells. *Culberson-Stowers collection*

Left: Culberson-Stowers collection

145

CULBERSON CHEVROLET INC.
1930–1965

Culberson-Stowers collection

Havoline oil in the six-cylinder engines because it caused an oil consumption problem, and it caused lifters to stick. We would add additives to them, but if we found the engine had Havoline, we would change the oil, and the lifters would stop sticking. It didn't make much difference which oil we replaced the Havoline with."

When Dick shifted to the sales department in 1953, he was allowed to be a full participant in the most anticipated activity of a car dealership—announcement day. People who weren't even in the market for a new car often hit all the dealerships in the fall just to see what new magical machines were leading the way to the future.

"It was a headache, but I enjoyed it, and I wish we'd get back to it," Dick reminisces. "Today, we've got several lines with GM at the same time, and we usually have cars from two or three model years on the new-car lots at all times. I kind of miss the days when we could cover up the windows, and everyone knew the new cars were coming. You uncovered the cars, and people really enjoyed coming to the event. It was a good time, but it was a headache. We used to unload the new cars off the railroad cars at night.

We'd have them all ready to go, and all we had to do was drive them out of the boxcar. It was only about three blocks. Our other problem was trying to get them serviced and ready to sell without people seeing them. We had to put the hubcaps on them, make sure all the fluid levels were up and the belts were properly tight, and wash them before we could put them on the lot or sell them. Those were fun days—days that made you stay in the business."

"We used to have all kinds of giveaways—rulers, yardsticks, balloons, pencils—and all of them had the announcement dates on them,"

Longtime Culberson Chevrolet salesman Paul Brown closes a sale in 1946. *Culberson-Stowers collection*

$1,095. Prices went up fast in those years. Now, we have cars priced at $50,000 and $60,000."

At the dawn of the twenty-first century, nearly half the vehicles sold in America are trucks or truck-based automobiles. But in the 1950s, trucks were almost exclusively rural tools. Culberson-Stowers Chevrolet was surrounded by the Panhandle's oil industry as well as by farming and ranching operations. In this type of environment, trucks played a substantial role well before they became the luxury vehicles they are today.

"We did sell quite a few of the medium-duty trucks as farm trucks all throughout our history—for hauling grain mostly," Dick tells. "In the '50s, trucks didn't come with heaters or radios in them. We had two heaters—a recirculating heater and an airflow heater. We only had one model of radio to install, but once they were in, it made the trucks pretty nice. We installed heaters in everything we had, and I'd say three-quarters of the cars we sold had radios in them, about half in the trucks. Most all the trucks we sold were the long wheelbase instead of the short wheelbase beginning in about 1954. People found out they could haul the most stuff with the long wheelbase. A lot of people liked the idea of going to a V-8 engine in the trucks in 1955. Of course, Ford had had a V-8 in their trucks for many years.

"Life was pretty hard for a truck in this area at that time. We had a lot of dirt roads and a lot of rough roads, and if a truck lasted 50,000 or 60,000 miles, that was a good life for them. Now, we looked [at] a truck the other day that has 490,000 miles on it, but that was all accumulated on nice, clean, modern highways. In the late '50s, we set up a truck center to take care of the big trucks, but that went away when we moved in 1965."

In the 1950s, the Corvette was heralded as a classic worldwide, but the popular car played only a small role in rural Chevrolet dealerships and no role at all in some. Culberson-Stowers Chevrolet has typically sold only three or four Corvettes per year since the sports car's introduction in 1953, but one particular Corvette sale resulted in an engaging story and a family heirloom.

Dot adds. "So many people came, and Daddy would get the whole family down there to help hand out things. That continued only a year or two after we moved into our present building in 1965."

Nearly all Chevrolet dealers recall the announcement day for the 1955 model as the most exciting of them all. That day, dealers revealed the Hot Ones, V-8 engines packaged in all-new bodies available in a myriad of stylish new trim and color combinations. Behind the wheel, the 1955 Chevrolet was the company's snappiest, most modern car produced to date, without the slightest hint of lingering prewar components. It was Chevrolet's first truly postwar car.

"I don't think I'll ever forget when we had the new car show in for the 1955 model in the fall of 1954," Dick continues. "We had the windows all covered up. We had a brand new '55 Chevrolet in the showroom—green with a tan top. It was the first one with the V-8, all that radically curved glass, and [all those new convenience options]. It was a pretty car. Somebody threw a piece of pig lead through the plate glass window and hit the hood and broke the windshield. It took us five weeks to get the car fixed. I was scared to death of that car because it ran $3,300, and I didn't think we'd ever be able to sell it at that price. When I first came, we were selling pickup trucks and business coupes for

147

Paul Brown officiates a moment of Culberson Chevrolet philanthropy as a 1948 Chevrolet pickup is given to the Pampa-area Future Farmers of America (FFA). *Culberson-Stowers collection*

major towns are 60 miles apart, comfort was a necessity. It was the Corvair's lack of comfort that troubled Culberson-Stowers Chevrolet.

"The Corvair was a different kind of car, and we sold a bunch of them," Dick recalls. "I didn't like the car, but it got you where you wanted to go. My brother-in-law had one, and he drove it [for about 30 years]. We didn't have much trouble with them. They were just a new idea. I think they probably worked better in a big city than they did out here, because we're about 60 miles from Amarillo, and I don't think people like to drive that kind of car for

"A guy came in, and we had a white '53 Corvette sitting on the showroom floor," Dick recalls. "I told him what the price was, and he opened up the envelope, and he said, 'I believe I'd like to have this car, and I'll give you this for that car right there.' In the envelope was this stone—just a plain stone. I took it to the sales manager and explained the situation, and he said, 'I'll be right back.' The sales manager took the stone down to the jeweler's, and when he came back he said we could take the stone and so much money for the car. We had the stone mounted and made it the company ring. Mr. Culberson wore it until he passed away. Now, I'm wearing it, and Richard will get it when I pass away."

Dick reports that the 1958 to 1960 Impalas were quite popular with Pampa's Chevrolet-inclined customers. The models were better riding and better insulated than Chevrolets had previously been, and they were more comfortable when driving across the Panhandle's long distances. In a region where

In 1952, Frank Culberson (left) accepts his award celebrating 25 years as a Chevrolet dealer. *Culberson-Stowers collection*

that kind of time. For longer drives, I think people wanted something a little bigger and a little better riding. It served its purpose well, although temporarily."

The Chevy II for 1962 fit the Panhandle a little better than the Corvair, as Dick explains.

"We did pretty good with the Chevy IIs. They were more of the kind of car the kids liked at that time. The Corvair was more of a family's economy car early on, but the young people really went for the Chevy IIs."

Pampa's by-then venerable Chevrolet dealership actually did better with the Chevy II than with the base-model, full-size Biscaynes and Del Rays. The introduction of the Chevelle in 1964 was met with enthusiasm by customers, and Dick Stowers agrees with other dealers who view the Chevelle as the return of the 1955 Chevrolet.

As the 1960s wore on, some dips and bumps in sales began to signal the troublesome times the 1970s would throw at the dealers.

As the turbulent 1970s approached, Richard Stowers was in college. He looked forward to joining the day-to-day operations of the family business. The OPEC oil

Ticking off the hours in the Culberson-Stowers Chevrolet showroom since the 1940s.

The Culberson-Stowers Chevrolet service department in the 1960s. *Culberson-Stowers collection*

The Stowers family: Dick, Dot, and son Richard.

embargo and the gas crunch affected the Texas Panhandle differently than they affected many other parts of the U.S. Chevrolet dealers in the area hoped the Vega would be their economy-car trump card.

"My sister, Suzy, had a green Vega, and I had an orange one," Richard remembers. "Mine was a five-speed, which was kind of hot stuff at the time. One of the first cars I ever sold was a Vega, and if it was adequately maintained, it was a good little car. The Texas Panhandle has produced quite a bit of oil and gas over the years, so while we had the gas crunch, and gas prices jumped, it helped fuel our economy."

"I don't like to think about the Vega," Dick Stowers laughs, agreeing that, like the Corvair, the Vega was less tolerant of abuse than most cars. "The gas crunch didn't have that much of an effect here because out in the oil fields, the oil companies still bought the same [number of conventional models] for company cars."

The gas crunch finally passed, and new technology reached family dealerships in the 1980s, much to the frustration of the eighty-something Frank Culberson.

"When they put in computers, my father only wanted to know one question: 'How do I look up the daily statement? What button to I push?' He had a banking background, and that's all he wanted to know from the computer," Dot remembers.

Dick notes big differences in the car-buying public today as opposed to the 1950s and 1960s, saying that while people were paying far less money for their vehicles in past decades, they asked more questions and wanted to be more sure of their purchase.

"Back in the '50s and '60s, we used to do the walk-around and show the customers all the features of the car," Dick observes, seeming to miss the past's more discerning customers. "Nowadays, we don't get to do the walk-around much anymore. The customers now are in a hurry to buy, and they don't want to hear the

Frank Culberson's activities scored him this Chevrolet Dealer Used Car Committee commemorative cigar box in 1937.

Frank Culberson, pictured in the 1970s, celebrating many decades in the Chevrolet business. *Culberson-Stowers collection*

stories about the vehicle and think about it. People now have an idea of what they want, and they want to know the price right away before they even look at the car. People were interested in details back in the '50s and '60s. For instance, if someone came in to buy a new Impala, they wanted to know what the car had to offer. They wanted to know about the engine—the displacement and so forth—and they wanted to see about the trunk space, the head room, and shoulder room. Most of them today don't even care about the engine. They know it's going to be a V-8 or a V-6, but they don't care like they used to. I had a couple question everything I said one time. They said, 'Prove to me that's how much leg room the cars has,' and they said that on everything. I told the salesmen, 'I don't expect you to know all the answers, but I expect you to know where to get the answers.' Some of them used to want to know exactly what the gas mileage was going to be, and I'd tell them you

151

can't prove anything on gas mileage because each person drives differently. It was an average, but they wanted proof of it. Back when we had demonstrators, I'd fill the tank up and let them drive the car to Amarillo and back and see what their mileage was. That worked out pretty good."

The dealership marched on after Frank Culberson's passing, and years after losing his grandfather, Richard still tears up upon certain memories of the man who helped form him and the business he's worked in all his life.

"My grandfather was about 75 when this happened," Richard remembers. "He was playing golf with a couple of his old buddies, and because of the way our local golf course is laid

out, they passed the pro shop, and they had about three holes to play before they would pass the pro shop again. There were a couple of young guys who wanted to play for drinks. [My grandfather's two friends] wanted to go back to the pro shop, but my grandfather threw out his chest and said, 'I'll play you.' On the last hole, he made a birdie, and the young guys had to pay out. That was the kind of guy he was. He loved people and didn't back down from a challenge. I never heard him [say] anything bad about anybody. He always had a good word."

Culberson-Stowers collection

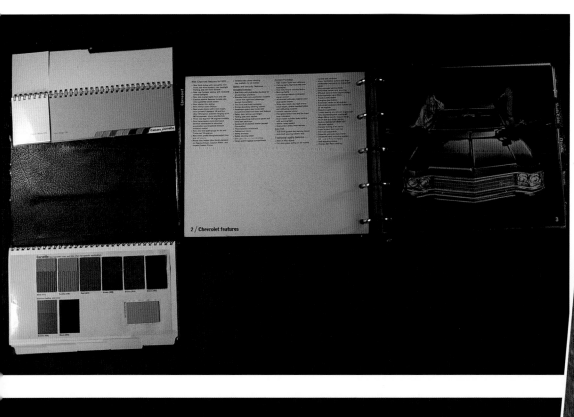

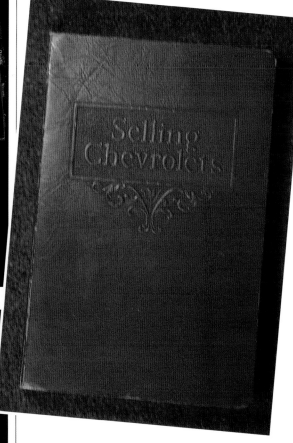

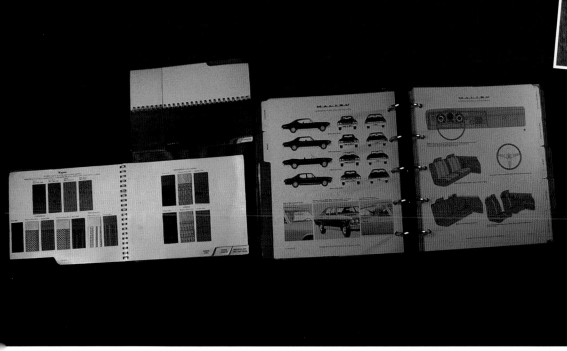

Culberson-Stowers Chevrolet has a better-than-average
collection of tools of the past.

Blanck Chevrolet

Like many dealerships that began their lives in the jazz age, Blanck Chevrolet of Brownsburg, Indiana, started out as an auto repair garage selling cars on the side. Edward Blanck Sr. entrenched himself in the automobile business when he was only 16 years old, working for a Stutz dealer in Indianapolis in 1914; working for Kelly Chevrolet in Greenwood, Indiana; and operating his own repair garage in between. Blanck became a Chevrolet dealer at this garage in 1928. This photo, obviously taken in the late 1940s, may have been a nostalgia shot for the dealership's 20th anniversary, considering that the dealership had moved to its Main Street location in the early 1930s. The photo features one Blanck Chevrolet service truck from the 1920s, one from the 1930s, and one from the 1940s. Edward Blanck Sr. is leaning against the white example at the right. *Blanck Chevrolet collection*

Blank Chevrolet moved to this location in 1931, just as the Hunter Bank in Brownsburg suddenly shut down. The fallout left Blanck with $7.50 to his name and only two cars to sell. To keep the doors open, Blanck Chevrolet also sold Frigidaire refrigerators and the Maytag washing machines seen in the windows. An ad in the window highlights Wype Auto Enamel, proclaiming, "Paint your car for only $3.95." *Blanck Chevrolet collection*

154

Bibliography

Chappell, Pat. *Standard Catalog of Chevrolet 1911-1990*. Iola, Wisconsin: Krause Publications, 1990.

Chevrolet Chronicle. Auto Editors of Consumer Guide. Lincolnwood, Illinois: Publications International, Ltd., 2002.

Dammann, Mark. *Seventy-five Years of Chevrolet*. Osceola, Wisconsin: MBI Publishing Company, 1992.

Garrett, Franklin M. *Atlanta and Its Environs*. Athens, Georgia: University of Georgia Press, 1969.

Kimes, Beverly Rae, and Henry Austin Clark, Jr. *Standard Catalog of American Cars 1805-1942*. Iola, Wisconsin: Krause Publications, 1985.

Live Wires. Milwaukee Railway and Transit Historical Society. Fall 1999, Spring 2001, Summer 2001, Winter 2002 issues.

Standard Catalog of American Cars 1946-1975., Second edition. Iola, Wisconsin: Krause Publications, 1987.

Index